Remembering

PETER GZOWSKI

Remembering

PETER GZOWSKI

A Book of Tributes

Edited by **EDNA BARKER**

⟦A DOUGLAS GIBSON BOOK⟧

M&S

National Library of Canada Cataloguing in Publication Data

Remembering Peter Gzowski : a book of tributes / Edna Barker, editor.

"A Douglas Gibson book"
ISBN 0-7710-7600-2

1. Gzowski, Peter. I. Barker, Edna, 1952-

PN1991.4.G97R44 2002   791.44092   C2002-903160-5

We acknowledge the financial support of the Government of Canada
through the Book Publishing Industry Development Program for our
publishing activities. We further acknowledge the support of the
Canada Council for the Arts and the Ontario Arts Council
for our publishing program.

Typeset in Janson by M&S, Toronto
Printed and bound in Canada

This book is printed on acid-free paper that is 100% ancient-forest
friendly (100% post-consumer recycled).

A Douglas Gibson Book

McClelland & Stewart Ltd.
The Canadian Publishers
481 University Avenue
Toronto, Ontario
M5G 2E9
www.mcclelland.com

1   2   3   4   5   06   05   04   03   02

really close to him had his love and support in everything we did. And we shared his enthusiasms. It was almost impossible to resist, even if we'd wanted to.

We all miss him, but weren't we lucky to have had him here?

GILL HOWARD

Foreword

This is a book of celebration and remembrance. It was Doug Gibson's idea, as was the notion that any proceeds from book sales should support Frontier College and Trent University. Peter's family, his friends, his colleagues and all the people who appear in this book support both ideas. People's generosity in giving permission for their writing to appear was something Peter would have truly appreciated. He knew what it costs to write, rewrite and then start again. That Frontier College and Trent University will benefit he would applaud without reservation.

Having spent twenty years with Peter, I had a fairly good understanding of the effect he had on people and the contributions he made during his life. In the days after his death, the outpouring of affection and the shared sense of loss did make it easier for me and for Peter's kids. It seems that many, many Canadians understood much about Peter, valued what he stood for and cried with us.

His friends, colleagues, listeners and viewers knew him well, and that is reflected in these pages. There are many references to his shyness, his ability to listen, his intellect, his love for this country and its people, his omnivorous curiosity and, of course, his complete disregard for sartorial splendour. Those

Laurie Allan and Shelley Ambrose, all of whom I thank for their time and help and support.

Finally, a working manuscript was sent to Wendy Thomas, who copy-edited many volumes of the *Morningside Papers*. As always, she made a manuscript full of mistakes into a perfect book.

I owe special thanks to the people who appear in the pages of this book. You gave me a magic hat to wear for a few months. When I put on the hat, I could ask for anything, and everyone I asked would say yes. You gave your stories and photographs and songs and asked for nothing in return. You have given a great gift.

And who am I, and how do I fit into all this? I am Edna Barker, and I was lucky and blessed to be Peter's book editor for close to twenty years. I edited the last four volumes of the *Morningside Papers*, which were put together in much the same way this book was, by sorting through letters people had written to Peter – letters that were typed or handwritten, without computers. I also put together *The Morningside Years*, the two *Canadian Living* books, and *A Peter Gzowski Reader*.

Peter was my boss, my mentor and an excellent friend. As I say, I was blessed.

A Note on Permissions: For this note, I borrow from the best: "In preparing these papers, I wrote to all my fellow authors, using the addresses on their original letters. Nearly all of them replied, granting me permission to publish. But in spite of my best efforts, there were some people I just couldn't track down. Presuming they would follow the same pattern as those I could, I have included their letters. I apologize for this presumption. I would rather have risked annoying them this way than by leaving them out." (from *The Morningside Papers*, 1985)

Editor's Note

A book like this does not write itself; I owe a great debt to many people for helping me make it happen.

To begin, there was Lynn Fogwill. My old college friend Krystine mentioned her name; Shelley Ambrose provided an e-mail address; I wrote asking for help, and received a seven-page e-mail that connected me to many of Peter's friends in the Northwest Territories. I wrote to them, and they sent their stories. And so it went, around the country: from the artist who designed Peter's first radio book to the archivists who care for his papers at Trent University; from Peter's television producers and his newspaper editors to people he cooked with, went to school with, played golf with. I tried to find everyone who might have a story to tell; I apologize to anyone who has been missed.

I also used letters sent to *This Morning* and to the CBC's Gzowski tribute web site. This would not have been possible without the help of the inestimable Laurie Allan, who navigated the murky waters of the CBC. And Rosemary Hillary transcribed two hours of *Cross-Country Check-Up* and *This Morning*'s special tribute program.

Once the stories and letters and poems were collected and shaped into a rough manuscript, they underwent the scrutiny of the Editorial Committee: Alison Gzowski, Gill Howard,

Table of Contents

Introduction

Remembering Pete

I can't recall the first time I met Peter. I know it was at a book launch because Peter told me it was. But I do remember the second time. I was hosting the local Toronto CBC morning show. The station, CBL, was a former movie theatre in the old neighbourhood known as Cabbagetown. CBL was a seedy place, though not without charm or history. It was next door to a notorious watering hole called The Winchester, and from time to time patrons of The Winnie would wander in, right up to our open-air studio, and hurl invective or sing.

The second time I met Peter was on a morning in late May. I was going to interview Peter about a scheme he had to raise awareness about (and some money for, he hoped) literacy. He planned to host an invitational golf tournament and give the profits to Frontier College, Canada's largest literacy network (and, in a lovely connection to Pete, one of the beneficiaries of the profits from the sale of the book you are now holding in your hands). It was 5:30 in the morning. My heart was racing as I awaited his arrival. He came in through the glass doors of the old theatre. The sun had risen, and light was pouring through the glass. I looked up and saw a silhouette of a tall man, ever so slightly stooped, carrying a briefcase in his left hand. There seemed to be a halo around him. I thought it was backlighting from the sun, but it was cigarette smoke – in those days you could still smoke in the workplace.

And there was Peter walking down the aisle.

It hit me then that I was going to interview the great interviewer. I was nervous – very nervous. I said good morning and expressed my anxiety. Then, as he so often did in his interviews, he said the perfect thing.

"That's silly. How many guys are you going to interview today who have a hole in their sweater?" I blushed, looked at the ground – and at his feet, which stuck out of hemless grey pants. He added, "Or have forgotten their socks?" I laughed and said, "Yeah, but I still feel like this is Oz coming to Dorothy."

We got into the body of our conversation: Why literacy? Peter related some statistics. How did you become involved? Peter told me the story of the cocktail napkin (which you can read about in John O'Leary's remembrance). And then (and to this day I don't know what came over me) I said, "Why golf? I hear as a golfer you'd make a fine broadcaster." He puffed up his chest and replied that, ahem, not only was he a fine golfer, he knew Canada's great golfer George Knudson. And then he asked me how my own golf game was. I puffed up my chest and told him golf flowed in my veins: my grandmother won the Women's Canadian Open in 1937, the first time in years that a Canadian had won it. (This is true.) Peter invited me to play in the tournament. We wrapped the interview. He stepped down from the table, said goodbye, clutched his briefcase and became a silhouette once more.

I was lucky to know him. He was a colleague, a mentor and a friend. I know I would not be doing what I'm doing today were it not for Pete. And what I'm doing today started with his invitation to read the listener mail with him on *Morningside*. When my union went on strike in 1989 and I was sans pay-cheque for a while, he asked if I would be part of the editorial committee for the latest collection of *Morningside* letters. A few years later, he asked me to write the introduction to *The Fifth (and Probably Last) Morningside Papers*. I told him I knew how to write for radio, but I didn't think I could write for print, so thanks but no thanks. What he said to me was too impolite to be recorded here.

I did write it. He edited it. And he wrote one of his memos, banged out on his beloved Remington on yellow paper. It begins, "Shelagh . . . it's lovely and whoever had the idea of having you write it is a very clever fellow. I have some thoughts, though." Boy, did he ever. His "thoughts" continued for two pages, and many of them were expressed in the world's longest sentences (see Bonnie Baker Cowan's essay). He con-cluded, "I like this piece very much and trust you won't find these thoughts anything but helpful."

A few years after that came the offer to be his permanent replacement host. Deputy host, as he called it. Peter was right when he called being the host of *Morningside* the best job in the country. The next best was filling in for him.

∾

If I can't remember the first time I saw Peter, I can easily bring to mind the last. It was in December 2001, and he was coming in to be interviewed about his book *A Peter Gzowski Reader*. He came to the office that had once been his wearing a white shirt, pink sweater and grey pants, hems intact, shoes with socks. He was attached, as he had been for much of the last few months, to his oxygen machine. He looked fragile. I felt a nervousness around him that I hadn't felt for years. He came into the studio, remarking that he should be sitting in the chair facing the control room. I was ready for him with the world's longest introductory sentence. He laughed, and I realized then there was nothing in the world better than making Peter Gzowski laugh.

∽

To date, the golf tournaments that first brought Peter to my studio have raised more than seven million dollars for literacy. Many friendships have been born at his golf tournaments, and some enduring romances. I think Peter's greatest and most lasting gift is connection. He lassoed the country together every weekday for fifteen years on *Morningside*. Thousands of people who couldn't read now can because of his commitment. I think of how so many of my closest friends are people I know through my relationship with Peter – Shelley Ambrose, his longtime assistant; Jenny Marcus, who co-ordinates the PGIS; Edna Barker, the eagle-eyed editor of this book (and most of Peter's other books); John O'Leary, the president of Frontier College and the man Peter and his Gill tried to set me up with; Alison Gzowski, the writer and editor, Peter's daughter – I could go on. And will, to say that the morning after Peter died I hosted a four-hour on-air celebration of his life (it became a great Newfoundland wake, with song and stories and Scotch). At one point, out of the blue, the singer John McDermott said, "Do you realize we all know each other?" Every guest on the program – Dalton Camp, Susan Aglukark, Sheree Fitch, Frank MacKenna – we all knew each other through Peter. He was very generous with his friendships.

∽

E.M. Forster wrote in his novel *Howard's End*, "Only connect," and that's what Peter did, as you'll see in the pages ahead.

Only connect. As simple and as complex as that.

SHELAGH ROGERS

Gzowski on Paper

If you repeated the contest today to finish the phrase "As Canadian as . . ." the only answer possible would be "Peter Gzowski."

– RON KARRAS, Montreal

In 1957, when a five-year-old girl was murdered in a Toronto ravine, the crime brought out the worst instincts of the *Toronto Star* and the Toronto *Telegram*, then ferocious competitors. After the police charged a seventeen-year-old schoolboy, both newspapers prejudiced his chances of a fair trial by running stories that assumed his guilt.

The *Varsity*, the student paper at the University of Toronto, published an editorial by Peter Gzowski that attacked the newspapers and insisted they be censured in court for undercutting the defendant's rights. To his surprise, Gzowski's words reached far beyond the campus. A lawyer read them out at a meeting of the Canadian Bar Association, the *Globe and Mail* reported the incident, and the editor of the *Telegram* was outraged.

Unfortunately, Gzowski was then living on fees the *Telegram* paid him for writing campus news. He was fired and couldn't see how to finish university. But luckily a job opened up on the Moose Jaw *Times-Herald*, and he grabbed it. As a result, he didn't get a piece of paper from the University of Toronto until 1995, when he was given an honorary degree. There was more luck: The incident caught the eye of Ralph Allen, the editor of *Maclean's*, who later hired Gzowski and became his mentor.

Could a great journalist's career have a more auspicious beginning? In that incident (described in his last book, *A Peter Gzowski Reader*), he enacted several themes that later became central to his work. He expressed the decency and fairness that eventually won him the love of a huge national audience. He articulated what many people were thinking but hadn't said out loud. And whether intentionally or by accident, he did it in a way that drew maximum attention to the issue and to himself. One more thing: The editorial by that twenty-two-year-old still reads pretty well.

Gzowski loved journalism (while hating much of it) and loved Canada (while knowing all its drawbacks). He made a career of revealing Canada to itself – in magazine articles, in books, in radio programs, sometimes in television shows. He was the ultimate pan-Canadian figure of his time, at home in Yellowknife or St. John's or Calgary. And yet (this set him apart from all of his contemporaries) he showed little interest in seeing the world beyond Canada. He made his first visit to Paris in his sixties, visited London hardly at all and Italy never. He couldn't quite explain this, so far as I know. It was as if Canada were more than enough for him.

Gzowski was managing editor of *Maclean's* in a vintage period and editor, briefly, in a not-so-good period. He edited the *Star Weekly* in its last year, probably its best. He was a major success in radio and a disaster on television. In the mid-1970s his late-night talk show, *90 Minutes Live*, turned out to be the worst failure of his life, one that he took hard. Years later he called it "the stupidest thing I ever did." It was as if for some reason he was not allowed to have failures like everyone else.

He was a wonderful companion, amusing and amused, yet he could also be irascible as a colleague when he suspected that his team was doing less than its best – or when he suspected the same of himself. In public, he was always casual and professional. On radio, he loped without much trouble (so it seemed) through several thousand interviews. In print, his style was so clear that it seemed effortless. His radio programs often felt inevitable, as if this was the only way that a certain day's show could have fallen together. He made it look easy. It never was.

His passionate marriage with radio, and the radio audience's passionate devotion to him, stretched over more than a quarter of a century, though there was a long trial separation along the way. He did occasional radio programs in the 1960s, including an early version of *As It Happens* called *Radio Free Friday*, but he and radio came together seriously for the first time in 1971 when *This Country in the Morning* went on the air and immediately established itself as exceptional and compelling.

It lasted for three sparkling years, and then Gzowski was gone from regular radio (writing books, doing television) until 1982. That year he returned to host *Morningside*, where he stayed until he retired from regular broadcasting in 1997 and became a freelancer.

If radio provided his most appreciative audience, print remained his real home. As soon as he made his national radio reputation, he began turning his programs (first *This Country in the Morning*, then *Morningside*) into a series of books that gathered together everything from transcripts of his most memorable interviews to recipes submitted by listeners. He wrote non-fiction books, like *The Game of Our Lives*, about hockey and especially Wayne Gretzky, and *An Unbroken Line*, about the thoroughbred racing he loved.

Because books meant so much to him, he made the literary interview a sub-specialty and did it better than anyone else in the country. He brought to it a judicious combination of humility and audacity; while respecting the author, he wanted to elicit ideas and impressions that the author hadn't necessarily planned to utter. He also demonstrated his greatest skill, attentiveness, an ability to be totally present in the moment. If attentiveness had been an academic subject, Gzowski would have had a PhD.

In the book business, "doing *Morningside*" became the acknowledged key to success. Publishers said that no one else could make the cash registers ring in bookstores like Gzowski. In the unprecedented development of Canadian literature during the last two decades, he played a major role.

That same interest led him to his great personal cause – literacy. Year after year he travelled across the country for Frontier College's reading programs, raising millions of dollars with the Peter Gzowski Invitational golf tournaments. His regard for that charity was rooted in his grateful understanding of what books had done for him. He seems to have enjoyed life most as it was refracted through the prism of good writing, a perspective he may have picked up as a sports fan. The drama of sports was heightened for him when he read about it in the work of A.J. Liebling, the American master, and in Canadian sports writers he came to know, not only Ralph Allen but also notable members of Allen's generation, such as Jim Coleman and Trent Frayne. He could be as excited by a new writer on sports as by a new athlete. No one took more pleasure than he in the grace of Jack Batten's sports writing or in Allen Abel's sports column.

Cigarettes, the emblem of easygoing manhood in his youth, killed him. His heavy smoking was at first a curiosity among his admirers, then a legend, then a cause of deep concern. In the

Toronto Star column he wrote for a little while in the 1980s, he made his addiction public, appealing to readers for their most successful cures. Whatever they sent didn't work, and he continued smoking until a couple of years ago.

Finally he quit, much too late, and found himself suffering from chronic obstructive pulmonary disease. In an article, he described his situation, typically, with merciless frankness: "You have tubes up your nose and are pushing a rollator in front of you, a kind of baby buggy with an oxygen tank instead of a baby." He described his life as a smoker in a poignant and eloquent memoir he wrote for an anthology on addictions. It was the last article of any length that he produced, and the saddest.

As a writer or talker, Gzowski never lost his sense of insecurity, and after a lifetime's friendship I decided that was his secret. Journalists become ordinary when they decide that the job isn't hard, that you should never be frightened by it, and that a few good tricks will carry you through. Gzowski never saw his work in that way. He knew it was hard as hell just to be interesting; to be really good was even harder.

Once, nearly four decades ago, Gzowski and I were talking about a young newspaperman who was trying to write magazine articles. I said he was promising, Gzowski said he wasn't. "He doesn't think it's hard," Gzowski explained. He was right. The fellow never did write anything of interest, but he remained supremely self-assured for the rest of his career.

Gzowski knew the difficulty of getting journalism right and remained terrified by the possibility of getting it wrong. He suffered from doubt before, during and after his most remarkable interviews. He understood that, because all events and people are unique, every piece of journalism requires a fresh approach. That was an intimidating thought, but without it, Gzowski's magnificent career would have been impossible.

Others retreated into glib predictability and replayed the ancient questions. Gzowski couldn't do that. He was afraid of failing to meet the standards he had set for himself. All his life, he had the courage, and the wisdom, to be scared.

ROBERT FULFORD, *Toronto*

I came to my Gzowski fandom late in life, or at least late in his broadcasting life. I began to regard Peter Gzowski with awe and respect during the tumultuous days of the Quebec referendum. I was travelling in southeast Asia at the time, and among the few English books I was able to find in rural Thailand were two volumes of *The Morningside Papers*. I picked them up only because I was starved for Canadian content, but soon realized I was meeting a very important individual within those dog-eared pages. Gzowski filled me with both pride at being Canadian and shame at being an uninformed and apathetic Canadian. He taught me the importance of curiosity and the value of the love of one's country. He gave me hope that my generation would be the one to forge a peaceful and mutually respectful relationship between all Canadians.

TRISH CLAIR PECK, *London, Ontario*

Like so many of us, I first came to know Peter Gzowski through his radio and television appearances. And like some of us, I knew him also through his writings, which are, in my opinion, more important than his media appearances. Peter was a writer, born that way, raised in that school, and, until his death, still a practising and creative writer.

I first met Peter at a June luncheon at McClelland & Stewart to honour and promote the new books for the fall season. That luncheon was thirteen or fourteen years ago. He came up to me and asked, as though we had known each other for years: "Do you want to meet someone who knows more about Stephen Leacock than anyone else ever could?" I had never met Peter before; he seemed to know me and what I was doing – I intended and still intend to edit Leacock's letters; and I was intrigued by his statement. "Yes," I replied sheepishly, and we proceeded to talk about his good friend, Peter Sibbald Brown, his neighbour at Jackson's Point.

It so happened that the next week would bring Leacock's niece, the redoubtable Barbara Nimmo, to Toronto, and so I suggested to her that we head up to Jackson's Point and meet Peter Sibbald Brown. We met both Peters for lunch at the Briars, and we relished a three-hour conversation. I remember it to this day.

And so began a series of meetings at Jackson's Point, sometimes in Orillia at Leacock's home, sometimes in Toronto, sometimes, too, in Ottawa. And each time we met, Peter Gzowski was the same reticent personality, the same person who was more the observer than the participant, the same informed writer and thinker.

When his *Canadian Living* book was coming out from McClelland & Stewart, I was asked to write a promotional blurb for the back cover. I was honoured and humbled. Weeks later I penned my tribute: "Because of his stature as a broadcaster, we may forget that Peter Gzowski is, above all else, a writer. *Canadian Living* is a welcome reminder of his unique ability to capture in words his own public and private worlds with compassion and humour. His compassion is that of a caring and shy observer of the human condition, and his humour recalls the benign laughter of Stephen Leacock."

Months later, the finished book arrived on my desk. There was a simple dedication: "I'll never live up to your most flattering blurb, but never forget it either. What a pleasure working on this has been!! Gee, maybe PSB & you & I should even think about doing something else."

The three of us thought of many other projects that would await our enterprising natures. But now the trio is a duet, and Peter Sibbald Brown and I regret the absence of our leader.

DAVID STAINES, *Ottawa*

"As I remember it, the boys were playing hockey on an outdoor rink, and someone flipped the puck out onto the crusted snow. One kid clambered out to retrieve it, and found he could skate on the snow. The visible world was coated with verglas, a heavy glaze of ice – and the boys charged out of the rink with their puck and flew across the fields, into the woods, liberated, laughing, playing hockey in the whole landscape, skating everywhere in a world magically transformed into a playground just for them."

I read that lovely little memoir by Peter Gzowski about thirty-five years ago, when I was a graduate student in England and magazines were among my few links to Canada. It was probably my first encounter with Gzowski, and I remember it vividly. I met Gzowski a couple of years later, when I was an editor with *The Mysterious East*, an alternative magazine in Fredericton. He was the editor of the *Star Weekly*, and we were both encouraging Senator Keith Davey to castigate the growing concentration of media ownership.

After the *Star Weekly* was killed, *The Mysterious East* invited Gzowski to help transform our magazine into the centrepiece of a school of journalism, with Gzowski as director, an offer he considered very seriously. Phoning his wife from his hotel room, he remarked that being in Fredericton "feels like being in Canada again."

But then came *This Country in the Morning*. I remember telling Peter that I couldn't imagine how anyone could survive fifteen hours a week of national radio for long. True, Peter had an unsurpassed intelligence and curiosity, and an endlessly seductive personality. But that assignment would eat a journalist alive. The host would tire of the job, and the public would tire of the host. Gzowski nodded.

"I'm only going to do it for a year or two," he said. "After that I'll be in the book business. I'm working on a book on Dow Chemical. . . ."

How little we knew.

When I left academic work in 1971, the CBC could still afford freelancers. A whole team of journalists was busily discovering Canada – Harry Bruce, Walter Stewart, Robert Fulford, Sandy Ross, David Lewis Stein and many, many more. One way or another, we all reported to Peter Gzowski, the de facto captain of the team. On *This Country*, *Morningside* and *90 Minutes Live*, I talked with Peter in Halifax, Fredericton, Toronto, Vancouver, phoned in from Bathurst, Guysborough, Sydney, Conception Bay, D'Escousse. So did dozens of other freelancers and thousands of other Canadians, and together we built a mosaic of a country we hardly knew.

Our generation had been raised, you see, in a nation invisible to itself, overshadowed by the gilded pomp of Britain on one side, and the brash power of the United States on the other. In our youth, as Fulford once remarked, Canada was a place that gifted people graduated from. But our generation was mesmerized by the brand-new Canada revealed by Centennial Year and Expo 67. The incarnation of the new Canada was Pierre Trudeau, the most enchanting leader in the world, a man who could not possibly have been formed anywhere else. Even when he was behaving abominably – "Where's Biafra?" – he defined an era, and a nation.

This fresh sense of Canada and Canadians galvanized a generation of superb poets, historians, publishers, novelists, artists and musicians, all fascinated with Canada's people, its landscapes, its politics, its history. In the end, they succeeded internationally because they were so intensely Canadian – and therefore so fresh.

Fulford comments that Gzowski travelled everywhere in Canada and almost nowhere else, and thinks that this set him apart. I'm not so sure. Many of us travelled abroad in our youth, but in adult life we were thoroughly absorbed in exploring our own vast, varied and little-known country, which simply interested us more than anything else.

As Harry Bruce says, Peter was relentlessly competitive in his youth, and he could be fierce and sarcastic when riled. We clashed memorably on at least two occasions. Once I panned a book of his; another time he jabbed me on-air for selling out by writing for *Reader's Digest*. But our friendship survived, and his last words to me, during a *Radio Cabaret* concert taping at the Rebecca Cohn Auditorium in 1998, were heartfelt praise of a song of mine performed by Doris Mason on the show. And by then he had no need to compete. He was the only genuine Peter Gzowski in the world.

His little memoir didn't say who led the kids on their wild charge across the verglas, but surely it would have been Peter himself – big, confident, sardonic and brave. That's how I'll remember him: as the captain of the team, joyfully leading a generation out into this big, cold, complicated country. And then the winter darkness fell, and we couldn't find him any more.

SILVER DONALD CAMERON, *D'Escousse, Nova Scotia*

Q: How do you edit the man who calls himself Johnny Canuck?
A: Gently, very gently.

The sobriquet was appropriate for the man who genuinely was more "Mr. Canada" than some of our founding fathers and many of our political statesmen, historians and authors. We were fortunate to have Peter Gzowski writing a column for *FiftyPlus* magazine because, as his health failed him in recent years, he was more selective in the projects he chose – a new book, a column for the *Globe and Mail* and a much-anticipated trip planned to Nunavut, one of his cherished places in the world.

For the past fourteen years, I have been one of Peter's editors and also one of his less famous friends. In fact, three days before he passed away, he called me to talk about ideas for the column that would have appeared in this space and to ask for an extension on his deadline because he wasn't feeling well.

Over the years, we had developed a friendship based on mutual respect but, more important, on trust. So, if I thought Peter should write a column about September 11 for us, he did. And when he thought I should get involved in his golf tournaments to support literacy, I did – although imagining the game in my mind was far more successful than the terrifying reality of playing with the likes of Lorne Rubenstein, who must have rolled his eyes in exasperation every time I hit the ball into the water.

As well as intellectual stimulation, Peter brought laughter and good times to his work and to his friends. At his famous Red Barn get-togethers before the annual golf tournament for literacy in Jackson's Point, he introduced individuals and groups who held the audience (and the bats above) spellbound – some of whom became international stars such as Prairie Oyster, Barenaked Ladies (who accompanied tenor Ben Heppner when he belted out "Roll Over Beethoven"),

Leahy, Natalie MacMaster, Margaret Atwood, Karen Kain and Stuart McLean. After a Red Barn, where the old wood floor shook with laughter and applause, we all felt better about life in general and a lot prouder of the talent this country has produced.

One summer about twelve years ago, a group of his editors reciprocated the Red Barn invitations in a minor but, as it turned out, successful way. Peter had written a column about the ten women he fantasized about as perfect dinner companions. They were, in his estimation, the most interesting women in Canada at the time. "They have cheek, irreverence and courage of their various convictions," he had written. They were Dr. Mary Wynne Ashford, author Alice Munro, political feminist Maude Barlow, Northwest Territories politician Nellie Cournoyea, ballerina Evelyn Hart, singer and comedienne Dinah Christie, Olympian high jumper Debbie Brill, politician Barbara McDougall, ethicist Margaret Somerville and lawyer Dulcie McCallum. So we invited them to a surprise "fantasy dinner" on his fifty-sixth birthday. They came, they dined, they luxuriated in good conversation and lots of laughter. And Peter, who had been fretting about Meech Lake and the future of the country that summer, felt better after a night of friendship and mirth.

He had two wonderful qualities surprisingly missed in all the tributes written after his passing. He was just as impressed with ordinary Canadians as he was with prime ministers, actresses, comedians and rock stars. And while he was the consummate journalist in print as well as broadcast, with several books to his name and an impressive stint as a magazine editor, his ego never got in the way of the respect he had for a good editor's suggestions or a fact checker's changes. He was modest about his writing and underestimated the power of the voice that came through in the cadence of his words.

In fact, when his first column for *FiftyPlus* arrived on my desk, I gave it to our publisher, David Tafler, who felt it needed some work and promptly rewrote it. Caught between a rock and a hard place – my boss and my friend – I held my breath, expecting Peter to walk away from the entire assignment. No one likes to be rewritten or have their thoughts on paper dissected but, while Peter didn't accept Tafler's rewrite – "Who does that whipper-snapper think he is?" – he did rewrite the column himself. Peter knew it didn't work as it was. He also had the grace to call Tafler and tell him that.

Peter wrote the longest sentences in history. They were as complex as his thoughts, as challenging as the issues plaguing the country he loved and the people he found fascinating. As his editor, I would often waffle between breaking up his sentences into manageable thoughts – hoping he wouldn't notice – and being honest enough to tell him, "I think I know where you're going with this, but can you get there more directly?" When I did ask him, he fixed it. It was a true working relationship. He cared about his work and appreciated the people who helped him polish it to its best. In an early column, Peter had used the wrong name in relaying the death of the artistic director of the Royal Winnipeg Ballet. The fact checker caught the error, and Peter subsequently wrote an entire column about the virtues of fact checkers.

This issue of *FiftyPlus* is the one in which we were going to put Peter's column on the left-hand side of the page. I argued for keeping him on the right, which, in our business, is generally believed to be where the reader's eye goes first. The only consolation in our loss is that we didn't finalize the decision. I'm glad. He may not be a "sir kind of guy," as he said in his last column, but neither is he a left-hand-page kind of guy.

BONNIE BAKER COWAN, *Toronto*

In the mid-nineties I was working as a clerk at Nicholas Hoare, the bookstore on Front Street in Toronto. I was kneeling while doing a routine dusting in the cooking section and heard a familiar gravelly voice from the other side of the shelf I was cleaning. He seemed to be whispering to a woman he came in with, but because I was so close to them I could hear clearly and immediately knew who he was. I slowly stood and peeked over the shelf to get a glimpse of a man I adored and was quite taken aback. Standing there was a smallish, scruffy man in poorly fitting clothes who looked not unlike the homeless people who frequented the store daily. Surely this couldn't be the source of that powerful voice that entertained the country every morning! I bent down again and listened. No, it was definitely him. He made his way through the store without speaking, garnering no attention whatsoever. I did not spoil his cover, but I smiled at my newfound knowledge. After he left I went over to the shelf that held his books, picked them up and put them on display at the front of the store.

KERI SMITH, *Flesherton, Ontario*

This is Chris Czajkowski whose letters about building a cabin in the bush were read in the late 1980s on Peter Gzowski's *Morningside*. Thanks to Peter I was able to interest a publisher in an expanded version of the letters, which became the book *Cabin at Singing River*. Since then I've had other books and articles published and have always attributed my easy start as a writer to Peter's continued interest in what I had to say.

But he helped me in another way, too. The publishers of *Cabin at Singing River* asked Peter if he would write the introduction. He agreed to do so, but asked the publisher for $1,200 for this service. The money, however, should not be paid to him, but to me.

Wilderness living, while rich in every other aspect, is always very much a hand-to-mouth existence as far as cash is concerned. That $1,200 enabled me to purchase what I had previously thought to be an unattainable luxury, a computer. I still live in the bush and use that same computer, powered by the sun, to write my books.

Thank you, Peter Gzowski.

CHRIS CZAJKOWSKI, *Nimpo Lake, British Columbia*

When the last *Morningside Papers* came out, Peter was doing a book signing near where we lived. It was just before Christmas, so I left the ad for my husband as a hint. On Christmas morning, I found not only the last but all of the books. In each one Peter had written a continuing pretend love letter, ending in the last one by saying, "Your husband is looking over my shoulder; I have to stop. Love, Peter." What a flirt.

JUDI CONACHER, *Toronto*

My first face-to-face with the man came in December 1993 when he was passing through Ottawa on a book-signing tour for his *Selected Columns From Canadian Living*. I lined up at the independent book sellers, thinking what a great gift this would be for my mother. Three hours later (who knew the guy was this popular!), I was about to have my book signed when I turned to my husband and said my mother had better appreciate this and the three hours I'd waited in line to get it. Mr.

Gzowski looked up and chuckled. With pen in hand, he asked me my mother's name and then mine, and proceeded to write the following inscription: "To Carol (Kim, who stood in line for three hours to get this, says you'd better appreciate it), Peter Gzowski."

KIM HUNTER, *Nepean, Ontario*

A few years ago Peter Gzowski came to Victoria on a book tour, and I was the reporter at a daily newspaper assigned to interview him. He would be waiting at the Bengal Room in the Empress Hotel. The idea of me interviewing Peter brought on a pretty good case of nerves. But there he was, smoking a cigarette and drinking coffee and being so, well, ordinary – how could I be nervous? My greatest difficulty was keeping the focus on him. Questions slid off him like he was Teflon man. Exasperated, I finally demanded: "Who *are* you, in a Canadian context?" He chuckled, stuck out his chin and said, "Me? I'm a cultural icon!" He nailed that one.

SANDRA McCULLOCH, *Cobble Hill, British Columbia*

When I was a nursing student at the Misericordia Hospital in Edmonton (1985–88), I was mercilessly teased by some of my fellow nursing students for some of the sayings I used, one of which was "Holy Nellie." They told me I was the only person on earth who would say something like that.

Well, I had news for them. Peter Gzowski used the same phrase, and I would prove it to them. I wrote him a letter, presented my case, and within two weeks I had a reply. Typed no doubt on his own typewriter was a little note: "Not a boring moment yet, Heather? Holy Nellie!" I was bugged no more!

HEATHER FERRIS, *Vanderhoof, British Columbia*

The only time I ever saw Peter Gzowski in person was at a book signing of *The Morningside Years*. My roommate had bought a copy for her father for Christmas, but she had to work. I agreed to go to the book signing for her.

I was nervous. After all, this was Peter Gzowski, the guy millions of Canadians had welcomed into their homes for years. Would he say anything as he signed the book? I anxiously practised conversations in my head. But when I got to the front of the line, I wondered why I had been nervous. There was Peter, his hair a mess, his sweater wrinkled. He looked comfortable and at ease.

Then I heard that familiar voice:

"Gee, an attractive young woman like yourself – this must be for your mother."

I told him no, it was for my friend's father. Peter signed the book and passed it to me with a smile. I whispered a polite thank you before escaping to hide my red face. Peter Gzowski had called me an attractive young woman!

Four years later, I was working at CBC Radio's *This Morning*. I never thought I'd be part of a program paying tribute to this Canadian legend.

Part of my role following our tribute for Peter was to answer the thousands of e-mails that poured in. Amid the thousands of letters were several that related the same story. They were all written by women, most of whom I'm assuming were my age, and generally began with a story of growing up listening to Gzowski, then seeing him at an event somewhere, and each related a special comment Peter made to her:

"Gee," he said. "An attractive young woman like you – this book/autograph/picture must be for your mother."

While it may have seemed to Peter that our mothers were his only listeners, the thousands of e-mails I read suggest another story. He warmed the hearts of many people. He was our tie to home, the voice that kept us coming back.

Thanks, Peter. I now know the truth behind the line, but you are one of very few older men who have made me blush – and it was worth every second!

LAURIE ALLAN, *Grimsby, Ontario*

As a CBC producer who came along after the *Morningside* years, I never worked alongside Peter. But it was great to meet him in person when we were both up in Iqaluit in 1999. I remember at the time he was writing a story for *Maclean's*. I was surprised to see he had written it by hand. He was anxious to get it typed and then have it faxed to Toronto. It was only about two pages, and I offered to do it for him. But what he really wanted to do was get hold of the old typewriter he'd used in his trips up North in years past and type it himself. So we went looking for Peter's old typewriter. There we were in this huge dark and dusty room with all this equipment that marked the many years of CBC North. And there I was with Peter Gzowski, the essence of the CBC and a well-known lover of the North. When we spotted the typewriter, he lunged for it. I remember thinking he was going to expire right then and there as he didn't even bother to get his footing before reaching out and swinging that old Smith Corona up onto a dusty table. We found a yellowed piece of paper, and he zipped it in and began tapping away. Alas, the ribbon had been rendered permanently limp, and we both agreed there wasn't likely to be another in all of Nunavut. *Maclean's* got the faxed, handwritten story. And that evening, Peter generously footed the bill for a group of us to enjoy a dinner of fine wine and great conversation at the restaurant adjacent to the CBC overlooking Frobisher Bay.

SUE CAMPBELL, *Toronto*

I first met Peter in the 1960s, and I have edited books of his such as the autobiography *The Private Voice* (1988); and I am proud that his last book, *A Peter Gzowski Reader*, bears the Douglas Gibson Books logo. I counted him as a friend. He was never easy to work with, if "easy" means automatic agreement with the publisher's plans. We sparred over contracts where I was shocked to discover that he liked to get his own way, and he was a perfectionist over the book's contents. He was, in other words, a pro, and I enjoyed working with him over the years and was distressed almost beyond speech when I first visited and found him with his walker and oxygen tank.

What do these books tell us about Peter Gzowski the writer? That he wrote well about his enthusiasms – hockey, or golf, or broadcasting. That he could turn his hand to an astonishing variety of subjects, from the perils of being dismasted in mid-Caribbean to the pleasures of family hopscotch; his last book, *A Peter Gzowski Reader*, demonstrates the range of his skills as journalist, essayist, narrator and polemicist for Canada. That he was, first and last, a writer.

Others have written about the glorious work he did for literacy, raising more than seven million dollars through his golf tournaments. I remember a crowded Saturday meeting at the University of Toronto where student literacy volunteers were gathered from across the country. Did he thank them and congratulate them? No. He ended his talk with the thought "Aren't we lucky – aren't we lucky to be able to do important work like this that we love?" He would have said the same to all of us who work in the world of books. And I hope that he would have said it of his own life and work.

DOUG GIBSON, *Toronto*

I met Peter when he was editor of the *Varsity*, the student newspaper at the University of Toronto. I was trying to be a cartoonist. It was 1956.

He came over one day and said there was a cartoon he'd always wanted to see done. Could I do it?

He set it up for me: A waiter stands at a table in a restaurant holding a very large tray. On the tray he's carrying is a huge, robed monk. The waiter is saying to a customer at the table, "You ordered a Benedictine, sir?"

I drew it. He ran it. Definitely one of the better cartoons that year – certainly the funniest.

Peter was a natural journalist. His gift was finding remarkable and memorable people and bringing out whatever was talented or memorable about them.

THE REVEREND IAIN MACDONALD, *Halifax*

I first met PG by leafing through the pages of *Maclean's*, in the 1960s, when it was the size of *Life* magazine and had line drawings of its star writers. There he was, with a Christmas-bulb nose, pine-bough moustache and goofy grin. But even then, even in that drawing, I sensed that Peter's twinkle was really like the glint of light along a weapon or a surgeon's glasses, and that he could be a fierce SOB.

I met him in person in the winter of 1977, when I was a free-lance journalist. An ex-boyfriend who worked on *90 Minutes Live* said PG's new talk show was a madhouse of testy, creative hysterics who just barely pulled each evening's broadcast out of the fire (sometimes not). The ex said Peter was the scariest of all. He had that attribute of most great journalists, a short attention span, and if he disliked a subject it was wise not to pursue it. He had, for example, announced that he would never again work on a story with the phrase "parts per billion" in it (he did, of course, but never mind). The ex suggested to the show's producers that I do a five-part series of live episodes on "The New Psychotherapies." So I was hired, and I lined up a quintet of Rolfers and Primal Screamers and a sampling of their patients to come to the Toronto CBC studio on Yonge Street. I don't think Peter and I talked before the segments went to air. I think I just saw him in the distance, energetic, rumbling and smoking like some not yet erupted volcano. The first three evenings went well enough, though I sensed Peter was restraining himself with the therapists and their fragile patients, if only because mockery and mastication, great in print, look harsh on TV. The fourth evening, a blizzard closed down Toronto airport and one of my gurus (was it the psychodrama guy?) could not land. We had dead air to fill, a show to improvise. How did Peter get through that night without strangling me? I have blacked it out. But I remember one of the patients I'd lined up made it to the studio, and he volunteered to play the therapist. We drafted a studio technician to play the patient. And there was Peter, watching with narrowed eyes as the pair demonstrated their therapy by beating the studio chairs with bats, calling out the names of their mothers, and the whole shambles went out live to the Canadian television viewers.

Maybe he blacked out this episode more fully than I, because we worked together again a year or two later, when he was working as an editor-at-large for Key Porter Books. I was hired to write a travel guide to Ontario. We went off to a boozy lunch to discuss the project. PG joked savagely that our proposed travel book would lure tourists to Ontario's wilderness only to find it had been logged out. He suggested that we include a pine-scented scratch-n-sniff card in the book: "If you can't enjoy the Ontario wilderness experience, folks, you can smell it here." My first draft was both sloppy and snarky. I realize now that Peter hated it because he loved Canada, and loved to communicate that enthusiasm. And here was a pipsqueak trying to look smart by denigrating Ontario's small museums and roadside diners. Instead of tearing me into little bits, however, Peter sent me a five-page single-spaced "fixnote," pecked out on yellow kraft paper. It was the best explanation I've seen of how a writer should engage in a conversation with the reader. It reminded me that passion for a place was far more interesting than cheap shots against it. And there wasn't a typo or spelling mistake in the entire five pages.

And then, in 2001, PG came to the pages of the *Globe and Mail*, where I was an editor. By now he was ill. At Peter and Gill's apartment, where we discussed his column over dinner, I found him dragging around an oxygen tank like a scuba diver – except that he was on the eleventh floor of an apartment building, not eleven storeys under water. He told me his lungs were so ravaged from smoking that they no longer sent enough oxygen to his muscles, and he could not raise his once-athletic arms above his shoulders.

PG wrote this last series of columns from home, pecking out the letters slowly on his computer as his strength permitted. He filed by e-mail and often coughed when we spoke on the phone about editing changes. Editing him was odd at first: There was a mutual acknowledgement of tables shifted. Me being deferential to him, and him being sort of deferential – or at least, generously unprotective of his copy – with me. Before long this odd dance became more relaxed. His column took longer to edit than other people's because we would spend so much time yakking about Canadiana, from the date of Ian Tyson's song "Summer Wages" to Peter's first meetings with Stephen Kakfwi, now premier of the Northwest Territories. I was sad when the editor-in-chief moved Peter's column to another section of the paper. We did an aw-shucks shuffling sort of goodbye, which took surprisingly long. We kept talking about how much fun we were having. "I'll miss you," I said several times. And I do.

VAL ROSS, *Toronto*

Peter Gzowski is firmly connected in my mind to food and its seductive aromas, such as the time we stuffed, trussed, seasoned and roasted a turkey in the old Jarvis Street radio studio so across-the-country listeners could share in the compelling Thanksgiving scent of sage and crisping skin – Peter did the commentary, I the basting. Another morning we dipped artichokes in lemon vinaigrette and nibbled off the succulent ends. There was the time we judged the chilli sauce contest, each jar offering up sweet, sour and spicy, and one morning we filled the new CBC studio with the aroma of onions and garlic sizzling in butter as I simmered soup for a man who savoured simple but good.

But the best food memory is Peter's beef stew. It all started with one of his columns in *Canadian Living* magazine. There he ecstasized about the sheer grown-up pleasure of making stew . . . trip to the butcher's to pick up the beef, stop at the liquor store for sherry, shake the beef in the *de rigueur* brown paper bag that held the sherry, his quirky preference for canned potatoes and his utter disregard for measuring ingredients. Times? Forget it: Peter's stew was a sensual ritual between him and his Dutch oven.

No sooner had the issue slipped through mail slots when the magazine received requests for the recipe – one with measurements so readers could duplicate Peter's or, better still, his Friday afternoon in the kitchen. The test kitchen obliged, transforming his charming "lots of garlic," "thick slice of butter," "splash of sherry" and "carrots and parsnips roughly the size of Brazil nuts" into precise tablespoons and millilitres. Later, following a tip from one of Peter's northern fans, we duplicated the recipe with caribou. Delicious! With Pam Collacott, Peter and I simmered up the by-now-famous stew at the International Wine and Food Show in Ottawa. And guess what – its fragrance pleased his fans there. While we may no longer be able to hear Peter's voice live, we can follow his lead: make his stew, and when it's ready to ladle into bowls, pour ourselves a glass of sherry, tear apart a baguette and get ready to dip our spoons into his fragrant stew.

Here's Peter's Favourite Stew

1-1/2 lb	stewing beef	750 g
1/2 cup	all-purpose flour	125 mL
1/2 tsp	freshly ground pepper	2 mL
2 tbsp	butter	25 mL
2 tbsp	olive oil	25 mL
3	onions, cut in eighths	3
3	leeks, white parts only, sliced thinly	3
5	cloves garlic, minced	5

1 tsp	dried oregano	5 mL
1/2 tsp	dried basil	2 mL
1	bay leaf	1
1	can (10 oz/284 mL) beef broth, undiluted	1
1 cup	water	250 mL
1/2 cup	sherry	125 mL
4	carrots, cut into chunks	4
1	can (19 oz/540 mL) tomatoes, undrained and roughly chopped	
4	parsnips, cut into chunks	4
1	can (19 oz/540 mL) whole peeled potatoes salt and pepper	

Trim excess fat from beef; cut into 1-1/2-inch (4 cm) cubes. In large bowl, combine half of the flour with pepper; add meat and toss to coat evenly. In large Dutch oven, heat butter and oil over medium-high heat. Brown beef in batches; set aside on plate. Add onions, leeks and garlic; cook, stirring, until softened, about 5 minutes. Add oregano, basil, bay leaf and remaining flour; cook, stirring, until blended, about 30 seconds. Pour in beef broth, water and sherry, stirring to scrape up brown bits from bottom of pan; bring to boil. Return beef to pan along with carrots and tomatoes; reduce heat to low and simmer, covered, for 1 hour. Add parsnips and potatoes and simmer, partially covered until beef and vegetables are tender and sauce has thickened into a delicious gravy, about 45 minutes. Discard bay leaf. Season to taste with salt and pepper. Makes 4 lusty servings.

ELIZABETH BAIRD, *Toronto*

Radio Magic

I remember a time I was sitting in a tent in the NWT and the rain was pouring down. We turned the radio on, and it seemed as though someone had turned the heat on. A sense of incredible warmth filled the tent, and we lay there and listened to Peter.

– BRUCE SKILLITER, Kindersley, Saskatchewan

I was in love with him, of course. Wasn't every stay-at-home mother? Even after the children were grown, he was there. In fact, I was a grandmother five times before he retired from Morningside. I missed him then and I miss him now.

– VALERIE WALKER, Calgary

What made Peter so good at what he did on Morningside? You could hear him listening.

– PETER H. BREAU, Shediac, New Brunswick

Peter's first show on radio was *Radio Free Friday* – a precursor to the daily show *As It Happens*. One Friday evening as I cued up the opening theme music from the producer's chair in the control room, I looked through the soundproof glass into the Announce Booth. There was Peter, finally settling in his chair, arms piled high with scripts, a litre of hot tea in his hand. He sat across from announcer Maggie Morris, and the two of them arranged their papers and waited for the show to begin. A minute later, I saw Peter jump up from the table as if he were springloaded. There was Maggie Morris, diving across the table, undoing Peter's belt and pulling down his trousers! This, of course, was all being acted out in pantomime because of the soundproof glass. It was two minutes to show time. Did I have a radio show, or had the world just gone batty?

As soon as I got into the Announce Booth the situation, fortunately, became clear. Peter, trying to take the plastic lid off his cup, had spilled the piping hot tea into his lap. Maggie, a trained nurse, knew she had to get the hot liquid away from his skin immediately and acted with the decisiveness and speed required by the occasion. I asked Peter whether we should go to music – even perhaps cancel the show. "Of course not!" And then the theme music came up, and faded, and Peter was off, telling the listeners what delights awaited them over the next two hours.

At that time the show went to air at eight p.m., and it took six hours in the studio to roll across all of Canada's time zones. Peter, as I recall, hosted all six hours of the show sitting in a puddle, in his skivvies, his thighs blossoming in blisters. The audience never learned what happened behind the scenes that evening. What I learned, at this early stage of his radio career, was that Peter had the kind of professionalism that would serve him – and his listeners – well.

DOUGLAS WARD, *Ottawa*

For a number of years, Peter Gzowski and CBC were at odds. One top radio executive made it clear that Peter was not welcome on air. He was between *Morningside* and *This Country in the Morning* in what Peter called his dark years. His marriage ended and his TV show crashed; he felt sidelined and without focus.

In Ottawa, it was summer, and I was looking for a replacement host for CBC's *Mostly Music*. The show was about Mozart, Shostakovitch and the like, and I needed someone who could talk up the classics without being stuffy. Not many people came to mind. "There has to be a Peter Gzowski type out there who can do a classical show," I thought. Then: "Why couldn't Gzowski do classical music? God knows, he's taken on any number of things he knew nothing about and amazed both himself and his audiences in the process."

I made a call to CBC Toronto.

"No," they said guardedly, "he doesn't have a number here but you can call him at home. Are you sure you want to put him on air?".

I was dumbfounded by the question. I checked with media colleagues in Ottawa; they confirmed that Peter wouldn't be welcomed back to CBC Radio. That did it! I called him right away.

There was a very long silence on the line after I explained to Peter who I was and what I wanted. The ensuing conversation wasn't much longer than:

"I don't know anything about classical music."

"That's okay. I do."

"Someone isn't going to like this."

"That's okay. Thousands will."

Peter walked into CBC Ottawa, unsmiling, rumpled and tense. Very tense. He worried that he didn't know anything about classical music. I thought his message was that he wanted reams of research and background notes. I outlined the week's shows and, after answering his few questions, asked, "Peter, what do you need from us?"

His answer: "A typewriter and an ashtray."

Monday morning, Peter arrived in good time and, with barely a word to anyone, isolated himself in the studio, head bent over his script and notes. A half hour before air time, I suggested we might go over his script, which I had yet to see. Negative. What in the name of God had I got us into? Whatever it was, Peter didn't want to talk, and I was not about to insist.

"Ten minutes to air, Peter."

"Thanks."

"Five minutes to air."

"Yup."

"One minute to air, Peter."

Nothing.

"Peter, thirty seconds to air!"

Peter lit a cigarette, straightened his papers, looked up at us in the control room and grinned. "Let 'er rip!"

Cue music.

"Good morning. This is *Mostly Music* and I'm Peter Gzowski, your host for this week. On today's program, Kazuyoshi Akiyama conducts the Toronto Symphony in a program of Mozart, Mendelssohn and Krzstof Penderecki. Now, you're probably impressed that I can pronounce names like Kazuyoshi Akiyama and Krzystof Penderecki. Well, my name is Gzowski, G-Z-O-W-S-K-I. All my life, people have mispronounced and misspelled my name. This means that I know the importance of getting names right. So, for the next week, we'll hear some good music, and I'll get the names right."

Before our eyes, Peter transformed into a happy person. He grabbed us by the ears and took us on a romp through classical music. Like a salt-starved, land-sick sailor, Peter took the helm of *Mostly Music* and sailed us far from known shores, searching out the new and the interesting on his good ship *Radio*.

Whatever the Ottawa experience had meant to him, Peter gave due. And that may have been his greatest gift. He took a nation of self-deprecating people, a nation that lives in a big shadow, a country that feels uncomfortable standing in the spotlight, and gave all of us, individually and collectively, our due. He saw our bits, knew how to integrate them into a larger pattern and showed us the whole picture. Peter frolicked in radio. He cavorted in radio. He walked on water with radio. And I bet a dime to a dollar, Peter Gzowski now sits in front of a heavenly microphone with his head-set on interviewing God, who, minute by minute, feels more at ease about the whole creation thing.

JANE FORNER, *Mill Bay, Vancouver Island*

It was Peter Gzowski who came up with the perfect description of a radio interview. He said it was like two people paddling in a canoe, each trying to go in the opposite direction. It was Peter Gzowski who came up with the perfect description of the radio interview because he was better at steering the canoe than anybody else. The politician sweatily trying to stay on message and the author chirping the title of his book in every breath could feel the interview moving into the tall weeds with Gzowski in command.

Before Gzowski, the radio interview was almost a set-piece encounter. With the glorious exception of Barbara Frum on *As It Happens*, most interviews were dignified and respectful, predictable answer following predictable question. Peter turned the long-form interview into a fully charged and rounded conversation that had muscle and texture and vitality. It was an irrefutable technique, and in a major way it transformed radio.

CBC Radio in the sixties was in the doldrums. Seeded by the mythic BBC granary and planted in the shade of American commercial radio, the venerable old institution had lost its way. Listenership was anemic; programming was dull; it had become irrelevant. It was time to turn the thing around or let it go.

Peter didn't save CBC Radio alone. Among other innovators were Frum and young producers like Mark Starowicz. What Gzowski did was bump radio into a new compass heading. He had a vision. The vehicle was a nine-to-noon daily program called *This Country in the Morning*. For three years starting in 1971, Gzowski presided over a cockamamie daily mix of interviews, music, quizzes, audience contests, weird monologues and oddball comedy. Peter took the radio to the listener. It was brilliant, and brilliantly original, and it worked. With a band of aggressive and slightly mad young producers, *This Country* changed the way radio was done. And in doing so changed the way Canadians listened to it.

At the cottage, Jackson's Point, Ontario, 1996.
Photo courtesy Peter Bregg/ Maclean's

PG at work on
the *Varsity*, 1957.

Some of the team that put the *Varsity* together, 1956-1957:
left to right, John Gray, Douglas Marshall, PG,
Sam Ajzenstat, Janet MacDonald.

Host Peter Gzowski probes issues from woman power to Arctic sovereignty, talks with radicals, realists, newsmakers – and newsbreakers.

on **RADIO FREE FRIDAY**
live across the country's time zones

Fridays at 8:03 p.m.

CBC RADIO

Life before *Morningside*.

The original cover for PG's first radio book; in the end, the book was called *Peter Gzowski's Book About This Country in the Morning.*

The This Country in the Morning Book Peter Gzowski

PG's Edmonton Oilers jersey – a treasured memento of his time with his team that resulted in *The Game of Our Lives*.

June Callwood and PG, with an assist by Ken Dryden.
Photo courtesy Tom Sandler

In the *Morningside* studio with Eric Kierans,
Stephen Lewis, and Dalton Camp.

In the
Jarvis Street
Morningside
studio around
1985.

Kathy - Lavin -

Vancouver Publicist: Julie Pithers,

Afternoon — Interviews as arranged by Julie Pithers - sked attached

7:00 pm - 9:00 pm — Evening event at Vancouver Public Library Free
350 West Georgia St, Lower Level, Alice McKay Rm
This is part of Duthie Books' Civitas Series
Contact: Scott Baldwin,

30 mins + 40 max questions

Call Roy - re/stock signing in Vic at theatre

November 20 **Victoria**

8 am - Vicki!

Fly to Victoria on Air Canada 1513, departs 1:15 pm, arrives 1:40 pm — Pick up car Budget #21897

Victoria Hotel: The Empress, 721 Government Street

Call Melanie upon arrival

confirmation number: 29659

Thurs!

Victoria Publicist: Julie Pithers,

Afternoon — Possible interviews as arranged by Julie Pithers (sked TBC)
Drop-ins (sign stock) at Munro's and Bolen's:

Call Marlyn

Munro's: 1108 Government Street,
– Jim Munro

3:30 - 4 coffee - Virginia Careless

Bolen Books: Hillside Shopping Centre,
78 - 1644 Hillside Ave, – Mel Bolen

7:00 pm - 8:30 pm — Evening with Peter Gzowski in Victoria
Kaleidoscope Theatre, 520 Harold Street (Chinatown)
Intro by Rick Thompson, GM of Chapters $5
Organized by Chapters Bookstore
contact Tonya Joyce / Roy Macfarlane [redacted]
Proceeds to Frontier College

9pm - dinner w/ Marlyn + Michael

11:00 lunch

November 21 **Salt Spring Island and Nanaimo**

Pick up PG at 9:00 A.M!! 10:05 ferry!

12:30 start

[redacted] — Fundraiser for Saltspring Celebration of Cdn Writers

→ All Saints By the Sea ← [redacted] downtown Saltspring
organized by Kathleen Horstall,
Books sales by Volume One bookstore

300 seats + LDY doing sound!!

Call Jenny when leaving Saltspring.

Yvonne Sharpe [redacted]

A day in the life: a typical tour to publicize one of the *Morningside* books.

Anne Bayin's PG
Beaver, as seen by
artist David Shaw.

An autograph session on a book tour across the country, 1987.

PG and Gill Howard at a McClelland & Stewart book launch.

Hosting a three-hour live morning radio program is like carrying a refrigerator up the stairs. It's like blowing up a lifeboat by mouth. You get up at three in the morning and dress in the dark or in the next room so as not to awaken your partner. At dinner parties you excuse yourself at nine o'clock. You go to movie matinees with senior citizens or kids playing hooky. You start to think about sleep all the time, the way teenagers think about sex. The program is not part of your life; the program *is* your life. Peter Gzowski, in three years on *This Country* and then for a phenomenal fifteen years on *Morningside*, did it day in, day out, year after year.

This Country made him the most famous and admired broadcaster in Canada, better known than the Governor General. When he left for television in 1974, I was plucked from the editorial board of the *Toronto Star* and given the job of replacing the icon. It was like trying to replace Dave Keon as captain of the Leafs.

Peter and I had parallel though not contemporary careers. Small-town newspapers, magazines, radio here and there. But he was the icon; I was the upstart. He did things on the radio that would have been folly for anyone to try to imitate. His connection with the listener was at once immediate and intimate. He could – when he had to and it was not often – disguise or hide his boredom; boredom, never disdain. I could not. He radiated curiosity like the electric element of a stove. It was real. He genuinely wanted to know how the young girl in Gimli carried off the blue ribbon at the fall fair for her pickle relish. His enthusiasms were never forced, his compliments never rehearsed.

In the very early going of my tenure, the differences between the veteran and the new voice became embarrassingly obvious. He was warm and cuddly. I was edgy and confrontational. He was rural, small-town Canada. I was urban, big-ugly city. He was Uncle Friendly. I was Mister Meanie. When I was fired at the end of the first season, it was something of a relief.

Radio can reveal a lot or a little about a person depending on the confluence of a number of variables. The inflection in the voice, the response to a dumb answer, the pitch and texture of the way you read a script. Everything is nuanced, and it is the relationship between the listener and the host that makes those nuances accessible and understandable. In his years behind the mike, Peter revealed a lot about the country and his love of it and his knowledge of it. But he didn't reveal an awful lot about himself.

Warm, engaged and affectionate on the radio, off air he could be brusque, aloof, remote. In fact, he was extremely shy. When I first met him, I was surprised at his physical mannerisms. I had expected him to stride down the hall in big lusty steps, swinging his arms and smiling broadly. In fact, he kind of shambled, shoulders hunched, head down, walking like a man wearing slippers.

Peter was highly competitive, even in his personal relations. He would bet on anything – a football game, a horse race, a by-election or the date of the first snowfall. One afternoon we were drinking at the Red Lion, the watering hole across the street from the clapped-out old CBC Radio building in Toronto. Peter asked me if I was any good at shooting pool. As a certified high-school dropout who spent many afternoons in smoky halls, I allowed as how I was not unfamiliar with the game. "Let's bet," he said. We agreed on $50 a game. I beat him four straight.

Repairing to the bar, Peter was obviously distressed. "Let's cut cards for the $200. Double or nothing." I had never won $200 at anything in my life and wasn't eager to let it go. But he pushed and we cut the cards. I lost the $200, then a further $200. I learned not to bet with him again.

Peter and I were colleagues, not friends. He was a complicated man, hard to know and not given to confessional conversations. When we talked, it was rarely about radio but mostly about our days in newspapers. He loved newspapers and he loved the newspaper life. In his heart he felt himself to be a writer. But his lasting magic was on the radio. It was formed in the little boy from the small Ontario town who hit the big city with ambition, grit, impatience, talent and intelligence. He made new trails, new pathways through the thicket, and like a little boy yelled over his shoulder, "C'mon, you guys, follow me." As Dizzy Gillespie said of Louis Armstrong after his death: "No him, no me."

MICHAEL ENRIGHT, *Toronto*

Having Peter interview you was a lot like learning to swim. He held you up for as long as you needed it, so easily and gracefully and unobtrusively that it almost seemed as if he was learning to swim, too. Then, at some moment, he let you go, let you take your own direction, trusted you to do it right. I think his listeners felt that he trusted them, too. He trusted them to take an adult interest in their country, to wish to be informed and entertained without condescension. And their response showed how their lives were opened and their days warmed by such easy courtesy, such comfortable respect.

He was a wonderful help to writers. Nobody was ever more effective in getting news of our books out to the people who might like to read them. I'd say he was a help to readers, as well. He was a help to all of us, for a long time.

ALICE MUNRO, *Clinton, Ontario,* and *Comox, British Columbia*

I can remember the exact moment my friendship with Peter began. It was in the parking lot of a Sobey's grocery store in Bridgewater, Nova Scotia. I was a young mother with two very small children. Their father was at sea. I was new to the community. As I pulled into the parking lot with my small boys in their car seats, Peter was interviewing two women on the radio. I can't remember exactly what they were discussing, but I remember the crystal-clear realization that those voices on the radio were my people, that this is indeed my country, and that despite my loneliness, I was not, in fact, alone. I waited for the interview to finish before I got out of the car to get my groceries.

AMY BENNET, *Big Lots, Nova Scotia*

In the early 1970s while stationed in Inuvik I worked part-time for CHAK, the local CBC station. Everything was handled by one person. Network hook-ups, promo tapings, music, local news and local announcements and messages were part of the on-air routine. Because of the coverage area, the Inuit and Dene population and the ethnic background of many local residents, the names in these announcements were unique. Omilgoituk, Kiktorak, Kimiksana, Avuigana, Kayotuk, Shingatok and more.

I will never forget the morning Peter offered, on the spur of the moment, to assist me with the announcements. We did fine at the outset but as we progressed Peter started to have trouble with some of the names. He got that twinkle in his eyes, that grin on his face and pressed on, doing his best to get the names right.

It didn't happen. He eventually passed me his share of the messages and left the studio in a fit of laughter. He was not laughing at the names or the messages. He was laughing at his inability to pronounce them. The harder he tried, the funnier it was to him.

Peter Gzowski loved Canada, and he had a particular affinity for the North and its people. This was always evident on his visits to the High Arctic. He would have been embarrassed if I had told him this but I have brushed shoulders with greatness. If this is my fifteen minutes of fame, I am proud to share it with you.

DAVE SHAW, *Glenwood, Newfoundland*

In 1981, I landed a job as a journalist and photographer in Fort Smith, Northwest Territories. I was a stranger isolated from the urban life I thought I depended upon. On New Year's Day, two months after I arrived, a drunk totalled my vehicle and I learned how to walk everywhere in forty-below temperatures, finding and photographing the news, spending countless hours shaping stories to fill our weekly journal. Along with the news, I also discovered Peter on the radio. Everyone at the Pinecrest Hotel coffee shop was listening to CBC (or Chee-Bee-Chee, as we called it); at Ib and Lillian's gift shop, at Kaiser's grocery store they were tuned in. In every home and government office, Peter was there, sharing tea, coffee and endless cigarettes. And he always brought the three things we northerners valued most – people, music and stories.

PAT BUCKNA, *Port Coquitlam, British Columbia*

I was working in Thunder Bay as a biologist in the summer of 1982 when Don Harron handed over the mike to Peter. Often

at nine a.m. I was in the lab with my co-workers preparing for
fieldwork or analyzing results. The news ended, and the
Morningside theme music came on – remember? Very flowing.
We whistled to it. But then PG came on with new music. One
of my co-workers, without lifting his eyes from his work, asked,
"How the hell are we supposed to whistle to that!" Needless to
say we learned it well, and to this day that theme music and
Peter's voice remind me so vividly of northwest Ontario and the
wild and exciting part of our country I enjoyed that season.

ALLAN GODDARD, *Almonte, Ontario*

I

When I was going to the University of Saskatchewan, I played
in a musical group called The Intensely Vigorous College
Nine. The "nine" is a parody of a marching band, we dress up
in uniforms, usually scrounged from army surplus stores, get
disgustingly drunk and take out the instruments to play – as
far as I know, the only similar group to us in Canada is The
Lady Godiva Memorial Marching Band from the Faculty
of Engineering at the University of Toronto – but they are a
pale imitation.

When I was a member, we were drawn from all sorts of fac-
ulties (which we lost from the excessive alcohol consumption);
but we were some very fine musicians – three of us played in
the Saskatoon Symphony Orchestra, as well.

In 1982, we were in Toronto and it was the last time the city
got excited about hosting the Grey Cup. By the time we hit
The Big Smoke, we were inebriated. Our first party spot was
the Royal York. The donations were rolling in thick and fast
when we met a guy who said he was a producer at CBC. He
probably was an assistant mailroom clerk, but what the hell – it

was party time. He said that we would be great on *Morningside* and he would make all the arrangements. "Just show up at the studio tomorrow morning."

So we show up about eight o'clock at the Jarvis Street studio and barge past the security guard. "We're on *Morningside*."

"Well, you're not on the list, but . . . okay."

We find the studio and walk into the control room. The engineer and producer are wondering who we are. Peter, who is conducting a remote interview, looks at us and mouths, "Who are these guys?" through the window between the control room and the studio. They go to a ninety-second local news update and we tell them what is going on.

To Peter's credit, he does not get the producer to call security (or the police). He and the producer decide they can give us fifteen minutes. "Okay, so we move the BC segment to after the hourly news and we can do the book review tomorrow." So the twenty or so of us are ushered into the studio, where we are interviewed. We play, we sing, we babble inanities; we were not sober so the exact progress of the interview is lost in the depths of my brain. After fifteen minutes, we thank Peter, he thanks us and we leave. Mission complete.

My only regret about it was that I would have loved to have seen the look on the guy's face who told us to go on *Morningside* the night before.

ROSS DRIEDGER, *via e-mail*

II

How Peter would have loved this!

I was the producer in question. We were halfway through the first hour when I noticed something odd in the adjoining control room. The curtain normally covering the glass partition was fully opened, and both the executive producer and senior producer of *Sunday Morning* were there. It was the middle of the week and most unusual to see them at such an early hour, since in those days *Sunday Morning* staff had marathon sessions beginning Friday and virtually no sleep until the program ended on Sunday.

I waved through the glass and all too readily got their attention. My sign language inquiries were met with less than convincing pointing to piles of tapes and transcripts.

Whew! No major breaking story. With relief I got on with the show.

About ten minutes into the second hour, sounds of a football pre-game show drifted up the hall and got louder and louder. I opened the control room door and reeled from the blaring of tubas, drums, trumpets and the odour of booze and sweat.

"We've come to see Gzowski. Just got off the train and came straight here," said the guy in front.

Oh, well, and why not? Jane Patterson, our technician, rejigged some microphones while we fiddled the line-up, and a bemused Gzowski watched some fifteen hulking guys, tubas, drums and all, cram into our small studio.

It wasn't the most memorable bit of radio, as it turned out, but Peter had some fun.

As they receded down the hall, I called to their leader. "What really made you guys come here?"

"Last night some guy told us to show up here – said he was a producer."

I spotted the *Sunday Morning* guys grinning a bit too broadly, still shuffling their tapes.

After much badgering, Stuart McLean, then executive producer of *Sunday Morning*, admitted to it.

Some mailroom clerk!

NICOLE BÉLANGER, *Montreal*

In 1987 my husband and I moved from Calgary to Vancouver. Neither of us had jobs; we had no family nearby, few friends and a new little baby to contend with. I remember looking forward to hearing Peter's voice at nine a.m. and listening intently to that morning's line-up of interviews.

Occasionally we'd get to the one topic I was really interested in and my little guy would start to squeal. Now I shouldn't be admitting this, but every so often when this happened I would fill the dryer with wet diapers, turn it on and set my son in his child seat on top of the dryer. Within a few minutes, the white noise and gentle movement would lull him to sleep. This truly must be the ultimate test for a dedicated, resourceful listener.

LEESA ALLDRED, *West Vancouver*

One of the most exciting days in my life was when I travelled to Toronto, to the Jarvis Street studio, so that Peter could interview me about picture framing and protecting artwork. Me, a humble picture framer, being interviewed by Peter Gzowski! Wow. I was very nervous, but he put me at ease instantly. Now these were the days when Peter was on that campaign to get rid of the word "basically" from the language, and I thought I had successfully expunged it from my vocabulary. Well, our interview was going swimmingly when all of a sudden that darned word flew out of my mouth. I screeched to a halt and turned bright red. Peter took one look at me, started laughing and put me at ease by saying, "My, you really are a *Morningside* listener, aren't you?" I will never forget that day, or that man.

MAR PENNER GRISWOLD, *Fort Erie, Ontario*

Peter's voice brings back memories of working at Harkness Laboratory on Lake Opeongo in Algonquin Park. Early in my working life, one of my jobs was to do stomach analysis of lake trout from the park. Sitting in a wood cabin lab, searching through the stomach of these fish and trying to identify what they had eaten, all the time with Peter's voice playing in the background. In the North, Peter and the CBC were life links that provided a sublime form of entertainment. Thanks, Peter, every time I clean a fish I will think of you.

BRUCE MARSH, *East York, Ontario*

I was doing something else, as I often did when listening to *Morningside*, and Peter announced that one of the items was going to be a skipping rope contest. I thought, who wants to listen to that? By the time he introduced it, interviewed the people and set it up, I was listening as avidly as if it were the Stanley Cup playoffs. For about five minutes there was this thump thump thump thump thump. I was sitting there right beside the radio absolutely involved in this contest. Afterwards I thought, what a genius. Who else could stage a skipping rope contest on the radio and make it interesting?

GORDON HEBERT, *Montreal*

Perhaps I'll never know where it came from. But when Peter Gzowski asked me the question, the answer just came out, and hundreds of thousands of people heard it. It was the morning of November 17, 1989. Friday. The night before, we – not just those of us at the newspaper, but everyone in the Miramichi – had spent hours scrambling to find out what had happened in the home of Father James Smith. He'd been murdered. We knew that. It was awful. We knew that. Allan Legere was the suspect. We assumed that. The rest was panic.

Then a producer from CBC Radio's *Morningside* called. Host Peter Gzowski wanted to find out what was happening. Would I go on air and talk to him? They could do it by telephone. It would only take five minutes. Sure, I said. I'll be here all day. Call whenever you like. It was no big deal. I'd been a regular on *Morningside* for some time. I'd drive to Moncton, sit in a studio and talk to Peter about what was going on in New Brunswick. I became known for my weird animal stories, moose that chased hunters up trees, runaway monkeys caught in malls. Those stories always seemed to delight Peter. At that point I'd never met him, never even talked to him on the telephone unless it was on the air. But so what? This would just be another debrief.

It wasn't. It took me years to realize why. Peter knew the moment I opened my mouth. Friends who heard the interview that morning told me later my voice, normally animated and enthusiastic, was utterly flat, lifeless. A friend from Vancouver called to say she'd never heard me in such pain.

Peter asked all the normal questions. What happened? When? Where? What was it like waiting outside the police line? How was the community reacting? I thought I was being business-like. Just the facts. Yes, Legere was the suspect. Again. Were there any clues to his whereabouts? No.

The five minutes shot by. It was time to wrap up. The problem is, I told Peter and the hundreds of thousands of people listening in on the radio, Legere could be anywhere. He could vanish, only to come back in a year to kill again. He'd killed four people already. We just feel so helpless.

Our time was up. Then it happened. Out of the blue. "I just wish there was something we could do," Peter said in his soft voice. "You could pray for us," I blurted. Peter signed off. I hung up. The moment I said it I was stunned. I've never been a religious person, to the despair of my parents and many a Sunday school teacher when I was growing up. Where did that come from? Friends called from around the country to say they'd heard the interview. A columnist in the *Globe and Mail* wrote about it. Now – years later, sitting in my office, looking at a photograph of Peter published on the front page of the *National Post* the day after he died – I know. It came from the place deep inside where there are no walls, nothing to hide your most private thoughts, your pain.

Peter was loved. People – even those who never met him – treasured what he did five days a week for fifteen years as the host of the three-hour radio program *Morningside*. I was one of them.

RICK MacLEAN, *Summerside, Prince Edward Island*

In the spring of 1991, I found myself sitting in a dank bar in Prague, Czechoslovakia, drinking vodka with a group of young Canadians who were in the country teaching English. The conversation turned to what we missed most about our country. We began with the usual topics – music, beer, hockey, Kraft Dinner – but finally settled on one common denominator between us all: Peter. Without an exception, everyone around the table had fond memories of mornings in university with a cup of coffee – possibly a cigarette – and *Morningside*. Now I'm no expert, but statistically I thought it unlikely that all these people shared such a common thread. As the conversation continued, it turned out that several months before all these people had heard the same interview inspiring them to travel around the world to teach. He created that possibility.

STEPHEN COUCHMAN, *Toronto*

In 1992 with much trepidation but a lot of ambition, I left my nine-to-five job working in a warehouse to pursue a dream. Equipped with only a love for art and design, no formal education in the field and no business experience, I hung up my shingle and declared myself a graphic designer.

Of course, as one might expect, the experience was best described as trial by fire. There was so much to learn and so much fear of failure that those early days in my tiny basement office were filled with great anxiety. The soundtrack to many a morning sitting at my desk and trying to create magic on a small computer screen was the voice of Peter Gzowski.

It was a most unusual combination. While I sat glued to my chair hoping that the phone would bring news of a company with deep pockets in need of creative assistance, and not another supplier demanding a payment, Peter chatted lightly with bush pilots from the north, farmers from Saskatchewan and prime ministers past and present. It was as if the world was sitting at his desk and delivered to my little office while my own world swirled madly about me. In many ways, that voice, that personality, those stories and ideas, the music, all became part of this new and exciting existence. It helped me to believe in possibilities and that, if nothing else, the pursuit of a dream –

whether it be as simple as my own or as complex as a country called Canada – was a profoundly human experience not to be denied or belittled.

That new enterprise became my education, and Peter became one of my professors. The course, if it had a name, would be Introduction to Everything (and I mean everything) Canadian. With a curiosity that was contagious, he explored issues and ideas and people as I would never have imagined. He was my link to the world around me and the country that was my home, even when my sole preoccupation was work. Peter's voice was there when I languished in failure. Peter's voice was there when I danced with joy at success.

I can call myself a graphic designer as it is now the position I occupy. Thanks to Peter Gzowski I can also call myself a writer, a cook, a lover of music, a golfer but most of all, and indeed best of all, a Canadian.

GRAEME McDONALD, *Dorval, Quebec*

When my youngest was born, I decided to quit my outside job and stay home with the kids. I was like many humble house-wives across Canada; Peter was the warm, friendly voice that kept us connected to what was happening across our country and in the world. I had a radio in every room of the house so that when I moved from room to room doing my chores (often with a baby on my hip) I wouldn't miss an instant of a *Morningside* interview.

One morning, not long after my husband left for work, I had just finished washing the dishes and my son was happily kicking his feet and making a mess with his breakfast in the high chair. I turned to wipe his face with a damp cloth. As I was doing this, the radio began playing the familiar *Morningside* tune, and Peter's voice wished Canada a good morning. At that very moment, my infant son, who had never spoken a word in his short life and about whom we had been fretting that he wasn't talking quite as quickly as we would hope, smiled at me, pointed his finger at the radio, and spoke clearly as a bell: "Gzowski."

He hasn't stopped talking since.

SUSIE DOYLE, *Timberlea, Nova Scotia*

Peter Gzowski was one of my best workers. As a building contractor in Vancouver, I counted on Peter to be on time, be motivated, be focused and keep everyone on track. He never let me down. Unknown to Peter, he was my personnel manager – I hired people based on whether they listened to Peter. Perhaps not the most sound logic for hiring a carpenter, but it worked for me. When Peter left *Morningside* it was like our best guy retired. Our job sites have never been quite the same.

RAULD LISET, *New Westminster, British Columbia*

Every third Wednesday over a period of seven or eight years, it was my pleasure to drag myself out of bed before six a.m. and stumble through the dark and lonely back alleys of downtown Saskatoon for my regular chat with Peter Gzowski.

I was a provincial correspondent for *Morningside*, Gzowski's legendary radio show. It was broadcast live from Toronto to the Maritimes and then successively tape-delayed so as to start at nine a.m. local time across Canada. The several time zones between here and Halifax mandated an appallingly early start for western correspondents.

The CBC's Saskatoon studios were then in the CN Tower. Access to the building before seven a.m. was through a maze of loading docks and dumpsters to a back-alley fire exit where I'd wait for the door to be opened by a technician with the requisite keys. Once inside, I was steered through a humming utility room, halfway around a deserted shopping mall, up five floors in a clattering freight elevator and into the dimly lit corridors of the CBC. Buying heroin would have been more convenient. And probably more lucrative.

In this case, however, the destination was a seedy little studio-storeroom where a wobbly vinyl office chair and a 1950s-vintage microphone awaited. Through a pair of Soviet-era headphones I could hear the corny *Morningside* musical theme. And then that voice: "Now, from Saskatchewan . . ." It never failed to thrill me.

What impressed me most about Gzowski was his relentless professionalism. He never stopped working hard to make it sound easy. He was always well-prepared. He was always thinking two or three moves ahead. He embraced the proposition that every guest was fascinating and that his job was to prove it. This he did, for every last one of an estimated 27,000 radio interviews. It didn't matter if the subject was a prime minister or a guy who made Canadian flag mosaics out of beer caps. Or me. He gave all of us his very best.

The Saskatchewan report on *Morningside* was fifteen minutes. The same as Ontario. Preparation was elaborate. On the Monday morning two days before, I'd get a call from a producer in Regina to talk over ideas for the segment. We'd talk again Monday evening, this time narrowing it down to four or five possible topics. These would be presented at a meeting in Toronto.

Tuesday, I'd get a call from a producer in Toronto saying what the two or three final topics would be. Later, there would be a conference call with a producer and the other Saskatchewan correspondent in Regina.

Tuesday afternoon, I'd be faxed a script and briefing notes. Gzowski would get these, too. He would thus know as much about the chosen topics as I did, and a whole lot more about everything else. His knowledge of this country was encyclopedic.

The script he never once followed. No more than Wayne Gretzky could have followed a script when he played hockey. The producers advised me to talk to Peter, as I was to call him, as if he were a dear uncle who'd moved away and wanted to know what was going on back home. No doubt they advised Peter to talk to me as if I were a doofus nephew. Could that have been his secret?

I did the *Morningside* gig for two or three years before I could sleep well the night before. What if I froze up? What if I yammered, as I sometimes do under pressure? What if I disgraced myself on national radio? If I didn't, it was only because Gzowski saw to it. A pro, he was.

LES MacPHERSON, *Saskatoon*

I listened to Peter Gzowski for years when I worked at Canada Agriculture. If it hadn't been for *Morningside*, there would still be bottles and bottles of unidentified insects stored in a back room there. As I met the interesting characters Mr. Gzowski interviewed and heard the wonderful letters of other *Morningside* listeners, I forgot the passage of time, stayed glued to my microscope, identified insect after insect and got the job done.

LESLEY MOFFATT, *Red Deer, Alberta*

My most memorable "sitting in the car while I should be doing
something else" experience was listening to an interview with
a guy who collected stamps. I couldn't believe I kept listening.
I have no particular interest in stamps, and the interviewee was
not an entertaining speaker. But Peter was able to touch that
man's passion and give him a safe place to express it. Who can
turn away from passion? I couldn't. And that was Peter's gift.

VALERIE LOEWEN, *Whitehorse, Yukon*

Peter was the genuine article. Even boring, ordinary stuff on
his show would crack me up. There was a great debate at one
point about the real lyrics to the worm song. People from all
across Canada kept saying, no, no, you've got it wrong. In our
part of the country this is how we used to sing the worm song.
And the great debate about Canada's national vegetable, the
rutabaga. The letters went on for weeks. I thought Shelagh
was going to quit the show over it, because Peter kept reading
more letters and more letters, even after they'd said they
wouldn't do any more.

MONNY RUTABAGAS, *Victoria*

I am not in any sense a public figure, but female lawyers and
law professors are scarce enough that I have been asked to
comment on this or that matter of law more often than some,
and thus was interviewed by Peter now and then. I remember
the interviews so well. He had absorbed every fact that I was
supposed to talk about; he had absorbed the approach his producer suggested. He sat very still. Then he asked something

from left (or right?) field that forced a guest to be spontaneous – to get over being nervous or pompous or stilted or "on script." It was unnerving but very exciting and energizing.

And then he did something even more remarkable. He listened to you, and his next questions always seemed to reflect what you had just said – not what the script prompted, but what the conversation expected. Finally, more often than not, he asked the "tough" question. Or rather, since he was usually very kind to interviewees, he identified the tough question and then gave you a way to avoid it, or not. It was quite a dance – and it left him both kind and effective.

DIANNE L. MARTIN, *Toronto*

I'm not one of the fortunate people who worked closely with Peter. But without his knowing it, he was always my mentor, the reason I decided to become a journalist and writer, the reason I kept on, even from Africa.

I was interviewed by him only once, a remarkable experience I'll never forget. As with many other of his guests, he took a nervous and dubious me into the studio and with his enthusiasm, curiosity and careful preparation, got me talking as though he and I were having a heart-to-heart chat on a front porch or under a palaver tree in Africa, with no one around to hear except the birds.

For many years from far-away places in Africa, I sat down in the heat and wrote him letters – from one Canadian to another. As soon as I wrote the words "Dear Peter," the rest of the letter came easily. I felt as if I were writing to a kindly and understanding uncle. Who is going to ask those unasked questions in that deceptively innocent voice?

I've lost that uncle with whom I used to hold imaginary conversations, the distant mentor who didn't even know that each report I filed or story I wrote, I would in my imagination submit to his rigorous journalistic eye. The loss is also for our media, where Peter's self-effacing style is so rare, and so difficult to emulate. And the greatest loss is for Canada – when I do return home next time, it will be to a country that will never quite feel whole to me again.

JOAN BAXTER BAMAKO, *Mali, West Africa*

After finishing university in the early 1990s, I found myself, like many of my classmates, un- or underemployed and left Canada to teach English in northern Japan. I had mornings, my favourite part of the day, free to read and explore but those mornings were not complete without *Morningside*, the one thing, along with President's Choice key lime cookies, I missed the most from Canada.

I still regularly corresponded with friends through the post, and one day a tape arrived in my mailbox. I didn't have time to listen to it before work so put it in my pocket. Early in the evening, waiting on a train platform in Iwamizawa, Hokkaido, I popped the tape in my Walkman to hear the familiar theme music and Peter's rich voice: "Good morning, I'm Peter Gzowski and this is *Morningside*," and then thousands of kilometres from home, in a landscape that looked like Canada but certainly wasn't, a friend was there waiting with me. I miss that friend now that he is gone.

ANDY WOOD, *Toronto*

My own special remembrances came during the early nineties when I was one of a small group of Canadians working in the South Pacific on one of the Canada South Pacific Ocean Development projects.

One Saturday morning shortly after I arrived in Fiji, I dropped by the home of a fellow Canadian, a librarian, who was going to show me how to shop at the local public market. She invited me in, brewed me a cup of tea and finished getting ready.

When we got into her car and started down the road, the radio started to play a familiar theme. It took a few seconds for me to clue in, since it was such a common thing to hear on my car radio back in Canada.

"Short wave?" I asked.

"Cassette," she responded. "My mother tapes them for me and mails a bunch to me every month."

"Can I borrow some?"

She responded like any good librarian: "I'll put you on the circulation list. I send them around to all the rest of the Canadians out here."

And so every week I would get a stack of one- or two-month-old *Morningside* tapes, which I would listen to while I went about my life in Fiji. It didn't matter that the tapes were old. The ideas and the stimulation they brought were as thought-provoking as ever. It was the voice of Canada.

HUGH WILLIAMSON, *Halifax*

I was driving out of my garage one morning in the summer of 1996 when the radio came on, and I realized some woman was talking about bloomers. I was poised to switch over to a tape. But then I noticed the voice was familiar to me, and so I stayed with CBC for a moment to figure out who it was. Imagine my shock and embarrassment upon realizing it was, in fact, me.

Peter has to be the only guy in the country who was capable of convincing distinguished academics and feminist activists alike to come on national radio and talk about their cheerleading pasts.

He was a master.

SHARI GRAYDON, *Vancouver*

During one phase of my life I opened a folk art gallery in Mahone Bay, Nova Scotia. This led to an interview with Peter. I was one of a few people gathered to discuss the nature and future of folk art in Canada. I was terrified, sitting all alone in the CBC studio in Halifax. What made matters worse was that the woman contributing in Ottawa was an academic of the worst kind. She had "just plain smart" oozing out of every pore, and I felt like an idiot – until Peter made me feel like the smartest person on the planet. You see, this woman had a high-falutin French term for the lawn ornaments we affectionately call whirly-gigs down here in Nova Scotia. When I said, "That's a whirly-gig, Peter," he started to laugh, and with that laugh the world just seemed right somehow.

CINDY SCHULTZ, *Halifax*

I'm a visual artist in London and I work in stained glass. I received a telephone call from Peter on the heels of a show I had at the regional art gallery. The subject matter of that show was Blackfriars Bridge. The catalogue suggested that the bridge was erected by Peter Gzowski's great-great-grandfather, Sir

Casimir (which turned out not to be true, but we both believed it). Peter was interested in buying one of these windows, and I went down to Toronto to hang the window in his apartment. He was in a Harbourfront condominium.

I had taken the hardware down to do the job but found I couldn't get through the plaster in the ceiling. We had to go to a hardware store. I was amazed how easy Peter was with the idea that we'd just get in the car and go to the hardware store.

Now the car itself was something else. It was swimming in coffee cups and memos and paper bags. You had to push the stuff off the seat to get in the car. The story goes that Sir Casimir, when he put the bridge up, sat underneath it as the first battalion walked over top, to demonstrate it was well built. Once I hung this window, Peter had me sit underneath the frame, and he took a picture and did a bit of radio about it the following week.

TED GOODEN, *London, Ontario*

Peter Gzowski and I crossed paths in 1974 when I was designing his first radio book, *Peter Gzowski's Book About This Country in the Morning*, for Mel Hurtig. When next we collaborated, in 1979, on Peter's unjustly ill-fated *Spring Tonic* project, he had switched from early-morning radio to late-night television (but didn't seem appreciably better rested for the transition). Somewhere in between these periods, I had come under the spell of a wonderful, obscure singer/songwriter named Gram Parsons. When I heard his song "Return of the Grievous Angel," I was caught – sinker, line and hook, as Gram might've put it. I learned that Gram had died of a drug overdose in 1973 but not before having helped launch the career of Emmylou Harris.

I went into overdrive searching for records and information about both artists. These were the days of vinyl and cardboard sleeves, and it wasn't long before I had a fairly impressive collection of records. The more I found out about Parsons, the more involved I got. I joined the Gram Parsons Memorial Foundation and designed some issues of their newsletter, *The Cosmic American Music News*.

But I'm getting ahead of myself. Parsons had founded a band called the Flying Burrito Brothers, which I thought had gone under in 1972 after releasing an album called "Last of the Red Hot Burritos." But in 1979 they appeared on Peter's show *90 Minutes Live*. Peter didn't have much to say about them, but one of his researchers admitted to having had coffee with the Burritos in the early seventies when Parsons was still with them. This was a gold mine.

I never did any more books for Peter because he changed publishers. But I learned more about Gram Parsons, the Burritos and other bands he had touched such as the Byrds, the International Submarine Band, and finally, the Fallen Angels. And the many people who were influenced in one way or another by him, such as the Eagles, Poco, the Rolling Stones, Elvis Costello, Jason and the Scorchers, Ryan Adams, the Jayhawks, Jim Lauderdale, Uncle Tupelo – and that list keeps right on a-growing, just like ol' Gram envisioned it would back when he coined that "Cosmic American Music" term. Shortly after his 1973 tour with the Fallen Angels, Gram checked into the Joshua Tree Motel and out of this lifetime on a toxic mix of booze and hard drugs.

I ran into Peter every now and then and always pestered him about giving Gram a bit of coverage on *Morningside*. I remember pulling out a best-of-the-Burritos tape and brandishing it at Peter once during a book launch at the Art Gallery of Ontario. But Peter wasn't taking the bait. Time marched relentlessly on, and suddenly it was 1993. I was listening to *Morningside* as I often did while working, when Peter played a song about trains and mused about why nobody ever wrote songs about buses. What? Songs about buses started rushing into my mind. The Who's "Magic Bus." The Hollies' "Bus Stop." Even (one of my obscure Cosmic discoveries) Scruffy the Cat's "Bus Named Desire." There were tons of tunes about buses. I dashed a fax off to Peter in an effort to set him straight. And never thought about it again.

A little later I got a call from producer Nancy Franklin. Our conversation went something like this:

"I'm calling about the bus songs – what's your angle on music?"

"I sometimes edit and design this newsletter for something called the Gram Parsons Memorial Fund."

"Gram Parsons! You're the third person to mention him today! What can you tell me about him?"

I told her a few pertinent details and mentioned local bands like Cowboy Junkies, Blue Rodeo and the Grievous Angels who I figured would probably all admit to being influenced in one way or another by Parsons. She said she would try calling the Cowboy Junkies and signed off. Later she revealed that the Junkies were already committed to recording a Parsons tribute track the day she wanted to book them. As far as Nancy was concerned, that meant they *had* to do the Parsons segment – the synchronicity was just too strong to resist.

The Gramfest took place as the very last hour of the very last show of that season's *Morningside* series. Gathered to chat with Peter about Gram and his deep influence were Blue Rodeo's Bazil Donovan, Grievous Angels' leader Charlie (Chuck) Angus, Caitlin Hanford (now of Quartette, then of

Chris [Whiteley] and Caitlin), and yours truly. We spent the better part of an hour talking about Gram's life, heroes, death, aftermath, and played a few of his records.

I never bugged Peter about Gram again. After all, we'd quite possibly given Gram one of his biggest moments of exposure ever. Almost a full hour of prime time on national radio devoted to a performer who had never had a hit record and who was hardly a household name. Since then there have been two tribute albums, and several CDs with lost recordings by Gram Parsons that have surfaced. Two books have been written and published about him, and the award for outstanding country music in Holland is called the Gram (it consists of a small bronze statuette of Parsons). A number of alternative country radio stations in the United States continue to air the songs that rarely got aired while Gram lived. But I guess that's what Cosmic Music is all about.

If there really is an Afterlife out there, it's got one hell of an impressive arsenal of talented performers and a burgeoning cornucopia of fascinating guests. And now – the perfect host.

DAVID SHAW, *Toronto*

Although I never sang about Peter on *Sunday Morning*, I did write a half a song in 1994. It was supposed to be for the newspaper awards, I think. Here are those lyrics, never sung outside the house, never seen by anyone else.

Do you think that interviewing is a piece of cake?
All you do is chat, well, how much talent does that take?
Okay, then, just try it once, and as you dry and shake,
You'll be in awe of Peter Gzowski.

Because he listens, he remembers, he connects,
And though he's more rumpled than a radio fan expects,
There are women out there who prefer his show to sex,
We are in awe of Peter Gzowski.

Okay, there is a problem if it's someone he admires,
He gets all touchy-feely, and his edge, it just retires,
Yet with the less exalted folks, he's brilliant, he inspires,
He makes them fascinating, Peter Gzowski.

Cause he listens, he remembers, he connects,
What he does with ease would make us total wrecks,
And if it's hard for him, no one suspects,
We are in awe of Peter Gzowski.

Pretty lame, actually. But see, I admired him, and that cramped my so-called style.

NANCY WHITE, *Toronto*

I can still see myself anxiously waiting for my name to be called to the dentist chair. Once I heard my name I could feel my heart racing and the sweat pouring down my face. The one thing I could relax with was the raspy yet calming voice of Peter Gzowski in the background. As I sat there experiencing various instruments protruding out of my mouth, I would feel calm as I absorbed myself in the conversations hosted by Mr. Gzowski. The topics moved me and kept me from feeling too afraid in the chair.

SUSAN MUNDY, *Lower Sackville, Nova Scotia*

My favourite *Morningside* show was Labour Day. I love routine and organization (funny trait for a military person, eh?), and Labour Day symbolized all of that and more. We are a military family, and I have experienced all the challenges of moving happy little girls, the Schnauzer with a heart problem and the air force husband with all his obligations. We moved four times in seven years, and each spring I would listen to Peter say goodbye for the summer and know that when I heard his voice on Labour Day, I would be in our new home, dealing with all those unknowns. From Sidney, British Columbia, to Goose Bay, Labrador, and points in between, Peter was my anchor.

I got lots of great advice and ideas from listening to Peter, but I think the best one was on how to cook a turkey. To this day, we take our turkey out of the oven one hour prior to completion, wrap it in blankets and let it steam-cook to perfection. Do I have to mention we keep the turkey in the roaster? The sight of this huge pile of blankets on our kitchen table has led to many a startled look on the faces of our Christmas or Thanksgiving guests.

PEPPER MINTZ, *Ottawa*

My memories of Peter are directly linked to the joy of Christmas. It was his voice that we listened to as we drove from Regina to Winnipeg, often in bitterly cold weather. I recall one year it was so cold that we were advised to keep the car running at Moosemin when we stopped for gas. We lived in Regina for seven years in the 1980s, and every year we would select a weekday close to Christmas as our travel day home to be with family. Our hope was that Peter would have a Christmas special of music and conversations. We were never disappointed! That drive with Peter was the beginning of Christmas for me.

DOUG EDMOND, *Winnipeg*

I am not at all a famous person but I was interviewed by Peter on his last Christmas show with Elizabeth Baird from *Canadian Living.*

I arrived early, accompanied by one of my sons and my husband. We found our way to the studio and there he was – Peter Gzowski! We sat for a few minutes. He looked as though he had slept in his clothes. He was smoking and hardly looked in our direction. Finally I couldn't stand it any longer, so I said, "Peter, do you know I have been in love with you for years and do you know that mornings without you will be like making love by yourself?"

It got his attention. He replied, "What's wrong with that?"

"Nothing," said I, "if you come from Dildo, Come-by-Chance or somewhere like that."

"Aha, a Newfoundlander," he said with a mischievous grin.

May angels cross his path with flowers.

BARBARA MERCER, *Upper Island Cove, Newfoundland*

Here's something I loved about Peter: He knew how to end an interview. As a radio listener, you get to know when the newscast is creeping up on a host and his interviewee, and it's so painful when the host has to stop the speaker in mid-thought. It makes me feel anxious to know it's coming – we've all been caught yammering on too long in a conversation, and the sympathy you feel for someone cut off on national radio is excruciating.

But Peter *never* let it happen. He had a lovely way of guiding the interview so that the guest could answer his last question without rushing, and he made it seem easy, as though any Canadian could go on the radio and shape a thought that gracefully filled the last twenty-three seconds before the ten o'clock news. He probably let his guests think they managed it themselves, but I think it was one of Peter's gifts to listeners.

ERIN LEMON, *Kingston, Ontario*

I was fortunate enough to get to know Peter through my letters to *Morningside*. He honoured me by naming me as one of the faithful listeners in closing the last show (I was Lisa Kowaltschuk for much of the time I wrote to him). Peter's biggest gift to me was to tell me that I was good at something I loved, which was writing. To have someone of his stature let me know he believed in me went a long way to helping me believe in myself.

LISA (KOWALTSCHUK) NOBLE, *Hastings, Ontario*

I worked with Peter Gzowski for seven years. And when people would find this out, I would brace myself for the question – so what is he really like? My answer was always the same: Everything you've ever heard about Peter Gzowski is true – the grumpiness, the charm, the shyness, the wit, the impatience and the intelligence, all of it and so much more.

I was the studio director of *Morningside* between 1990 and its finale in 1997. I described my job as the conductor of the orchestra; someone else had written the score and someone else was playing the instruments, but it was my job to make it come alive. I started every day at 5:30 a.m. Peter would walk in twenty minutes later, and together we'd look over the storyboard to get a blueprint of that day's show. It might look like this: Hour One: KCL 18, circle, Letters (SR) 5, circle, Signs of Spring Drive 12. That mysterious collection of symbols and letters would translate as Eric Kierans, Dalton Camp and Stephen Lewis panel, scheduled to run for eighteen minutes followed by a song. Then letters with Shelagh Rogers, another song and finally a twelve-minute feature with three phone calls to listeners who would give us their signs of spring from across the country. That would be the plan, anyway. But then we'd figure out how to shape it from a collection of interviews and music to an organic whole.

At 8:05, the show got underway. I sat in the control room and kept him on track as he steered the show. I made sure he had everything he needed so all he had to do was his job.

What did he do for me? The rewards were immeasurable.

One day we had a psychologist on to talk about shyness. He said there are extroverts and introverts, and those differences aren't as apparent as you might think. When a true extrovert speaks at a conference, for example, she is so energized by it that she can go on to tackle a big job right after. An introvert can also deliver a great presentation, but afterwards, he has to go into the end stall of the washroom and sit there for ten minutes to breathe deeply and be alone. Peter was the guy in the end stall.

So what was he really like? He was a man who was much smarter than he let on, endlessly curious about people, and in the end, as true a man as I've ever met. Was he perfect? By no means. Were they the best days of my working life? Absolutely. Will I miss him? Every day.

MARIEKE MEYER, *Toronto*

Every weekday morning, after three hours of live radio, a couple of cigarettes or more – in the smoking room down the hall, of course – and some phone calls, Peter Gzowski would shuffle, head down, into *Morningside*'s open office area, where the producers worked. You know, he walked much like he talked – in a kind of bumbling fashion that made it look like he didn't know where he was going. He did, of course. He'd sink into his corner of the sofa – like The Dad, he had His Chair – and balance a small carton of milk and a paper plate holding a sandwich on his knee, and listen. I was a producer at *Morningside* during its last three years and Gzowski's last years as a daily radio host. By then, meaning both by his lunchtime and at that stage of his career, he was tired.

As warm and as open as Gzowski was with his radio audience, he was, away from the studio and its microphones, a shy, introverted man. By the time the story meeting rolled around, he was also talked out. So he'd grunt and bark approval or disapproval of producers' ideas of what to put on the air. Gzowski would sit, and his pants would bunch up around his knees to expose his white, hairless and – even in winter – sockless shins, his feet covered with pale leather loafers. He looked like a man who dressed in the dark, which may well have been true – he almost always arrived at work before dawn. He wore sweaters – often for days on end – that, if they weren't stained or unravelling, invariably had cigarette burns. He'd bite into his sandwich, flicking the crumbs from his fingers onto the little plate, and appear uninterested, as producers struggled to come up with the best approach to a story or the best person to speak on a topic. But then, just when the discussion was really going nowhere, he'd speak up. "Why don't you try so-and-so?" he'd suggest, surprising us because he had been listening after all. And he'd hit the nail right on the head – it was the right idea.

While he wanted recognition for his work – he knew it was

good – Gzowski didn't like the adulation that came with being a star. I'd once booked a large panel for the show, five people from across the country as I recall, one of whom was a fiftyish woman who lived north of Toronto and was the only guest in Gzowski's studio. Before the program began, Gzowski emerged from his office – a small, book-filled space – to say hello. Well, she gushed and blathered about how wonderful it was to meet him in person – and, well, never was she invited back again.

Gzowski cared, tremendously, about his work, about his show, about radio, about the people he worked with, about journalism, about Canada – and about his audience. He connected with his listeners in a way no other broadcaster has managed to do. He truly listened on their behalf and used the incredible depth of his intelligence and the breadth of his knowledge to make stories come alive. His finely tuned bullshit meter came in handy, too. As an interviewer, he was master of the craft; he could spar with the likes of Conrad Black or connect with the longings of Leonard Cohen. As a producer, I'd sit in the studio, on the control room side of the glass and watch and listen to the items I was responsible for. I knew, by watching his moustache, when the interview or the panel had really piqued his curiosity. He'd twist and scrunch up his mouth, and his fingers – ink- and nicotine-stained, always – would dance in the air, as he'd listen and think about his next parry, and his bristly moustache would jerk and twitch.

The twitching moustache would sometimes happen in a story meeting, too, if Gzowski was excited about an idea. Yet once he'd made his precise, bon mot suggestion, he'd leave the details for producers to work out. With his sandwich done, and confident that the next morning's show was more or less under control, he'd lift himself out of the low sofa and, usually heading out for a smoke, he'd shuffle off.

KATHERINE MACKLEM, *Toronto*

In his memoir *The Private Voice*, Peter Gzowski described his method for reading the books he covered on *Morningside*. He wrote: "I've learned how to skim over a manuscript like a motorboat planing through the open sea." Now, most motorboats have a rocky time on the open sea, so there could only be one craft he had in mind: the cigarette boat.

The role of the books producer at *Morningside* was something like being a tugboat to assist that cigarette boat. We would clear the waters, tow the boat into place, and then watch it glide serenely through its usual fourteen- to eighteen-minute laps. It didn't lose any steam during twenty-four-minute intervals and it could handle fifty-minute marathons at full throttle. It was a sleek, high-performance machine, undeterred by the occasional ash on its sweater.

What fuelled the cigarette boat was a potent mixture of curiosity, respect and fear. The curiosity was obvious to any listener and sometimes frustrating to the books producer. The guy would browse through the fall book catalogues and want to do everything. If we had booked Margaret Atwood for Monday, Richard Gwyn for Wednesday and Mark Kingwell for Friday, Peter wouldn't hesitate at suggesting that we throw in that fascinating book on sea otters on Tuesday or Thursday. The result was good radio, but it sometimes meant a fifteen-hundred-page week for the producer and the host. The pilot of the cigarette boat never complained, but those of us who served on the tugboat – from Hal Wake to Larry Scanlan to Peter Kavanagh to myself to Paul Wilson – often had fantasies about what the people on shore were doing in the evenings. Occasionally, pods of singing mermaids would come to visit, but that's another story.

The respect was also obvious to the listener. Peter was first and foremost a writer, and he knew about the sweat and talent that go into a book. He understood that a few years of a person's work deserved more than the blurb treatment that books receive in most radio and TV spots. The long, attentive book interview is now a staple on the CBC, but it was writer Peter Gzowski who possibly invented it, and certainly perfected it.

But what really drove Peter was fear. Every time he spoke to an author, he was speaking with someone who knew way more about their subject than he did. He didn't want to be caught out. He wanted to chat as colleagues sharing a secret, and the only way to do that was to read the book. I remember leading Oliver Sacks out of the studio after Peter had spoken with him about *An Anthropologist on Mars*. Dr. Sacks was shaking his head in astonishment and gratitude and he said, "He put so much into it. He made it so easy. He was so generous." I expect that most of the thousand or so writers that Peter interviewed during his fifteen years on *Morningside* felt the same way.

IAN PEARSON, *Toronto*

There's a silver oblong on my key chain. On one side is printed "Morningside 1982–1997." On the other is Peter Gzowski's signature and "many thanks!" Enlarged, it could be the tombstone for the best radio program ever produced in this country, perhaps the world. For five years, I was its executive producer. About three hundred other people have the same key fob. It was Peter's present at the party that wrapped it all up.

I met him in 1973 at a CBC station in Thunder Bay, Ontario. He was there on a remote (a broadcast from a location other than CBC Toronto) and he was a celebrity. One day a local artist, a good one, came by with a tiny oil painting, an ice-breaker in Lake Superior in front of the rock formation known as the Sleeping Giant. She wanted Peter to have it as a token of her appreciation as a listener. I would later know this happened a great deal. She wanted him to come downstairs – his temporary office was upstairs – because she wanted to give it to him personally.

It took some coaxing but he came downstairs and, almost like a little kid, scuffed his toe into the carpet as he accepted it. I realized then, for the first time, that Peter Gzowski was shy. In his own words, from a letter to a Newfoundlander named Bill whose last name I can't remember, "I know I have a reputation for treating people badly. I hate that reputation even though some of it is my fault." In his job, he had to muster heroic concentration and flexibility. Sometimes a guest wouldn't understand an abrupt dismissal after such a friendly conversation. But Peter had a three-minute piece of music during which to make the transition to the next story, the next guest. It's not long, and he did it thirteen times a morning.

When people ask, as they do all the time, what's Peter Gzowski like, I say, "Primarily he's a shy, boyish guy who's unusually smart." The shyness didn't surface on the radio, but it was there on the telephone. Peter was awful on the telephone. Same process, speaking into a mouthpiece, different medium. The telephone is more personal, I guess. Very early in life, his dad left. His mother died at thirty-nine. And he had a condition that troubled him even in middle age, cystic acne. He once told me about playing football in high school. In his youth, Peter was a good athlete, and being in shape as a kid sustained his health for many years after he seemed determined to ruin it. He'd come in from the game, any game, and he'd know a place in the locker room where he could take off his football jersey in private. Two things about the process were mortifying: The pustules on his back had burst with the

activity and the sweater was welded to his skin. Removing it
was excruciating and brought tears to his eyes. His spirit and
his complexion were scarred.

As a writer, Peter told good stories. Elizabeth Gray, a few
years younger and a fellow university journalist of their time,
says the young Gzowski could make a trip to the laundromat
sound like an adventure. He could be breathtaking.

Years later, after the *Star Weekly*, *Maclean's* magazine, *This
Country in the Morning* and *Radio Free Friday*, he and I became
friends. When I arrived in Toronto a couple of years later,
Peter was doing a little – and very good – radio program,
Gzowski on FM. He and a bunch of CBC radio staffers, including me, played Password for hours at the Red Lion. Peter is a
games guy. I've stayed at his cottage on occasion, and you were
at the Scrabble board in your jammies in the morning. He
wasn't great at losing but he didn't lose very often.

In 1976, Peter became the host of *90 Minutes Live*, a better
television program than the critics thought but one that
required too much change of Peter. Everybody who remembers
it could see how uncomfortable he was, dressed to the hilt,
coiffed, shins safely covered. When it was cancelled, he went
into a spiral and became a recluse in Rockwood, Ontario. I
think he was having a bout with the depression that surfaced
every once in a while throughout his life. He took the public fall
for the cancellation of *90 Minutes Live* and was kind of ostra-
cized from the Corporation for a few years. I think I created the
momentum to hire him as a fill-in host on *As It Happens*, around
1980. But it was executive producer Nicole Bélanger who,
when Don Harron left her program, *Morningside*, made the
brilliant decision to get Peter back in the chair. He and I had a
drink sometime during his negotiations for the job, and he
asked me if he should take it. But he really didn't have any

choice, did he? He'd been waiting for the chance ever since leaving radio for TV.

The rest is history. A little of it included me, and it was a luxury to spend an hour or more every day talking with Peter. First of all, he was funny, black, perverse and most of all irreverent. We had a lot of fun. Peter had a great laugh. Fans will be familiar with the program where he and Stuart McLean lost it on air over a dead cricket. His daughter tells me he laughed at a joke just before being placed on life support.

Our conversations at *Morningside*: What have we been missing? How can we take this story forward? What are you thinking about this story? He came up with the lion's share of ideas at story meetings. He nurtured his producers, listened to them and credited them. He grew to like, with few exceptions – two, I think – almost everyone who came through, and there were many.

Despite his success in radio, Peter always considered himself a print man. He agonized over the fact that he never wrote *the* book about Canada. He was always going to, and that ambition was with him to the end. He tried. But it was too late. During sessions when he was beating himself up, it didn't help to remind him that while he was a very good writer he probably would never be the best, and that he was arguably the best radio broadcaster in the world. It's ironic that his series of *Morningside Papers* may have accomplished his ambition without his knowing it.

For five years I came to work most mornings to find a sheet of yellow paper (from what we used to call five-part canaries, the paper and carbon combination we typed on when we used typewriters – and he always wrote his opening monologue on a typewriter) on my desk or my chair. It was a note about what Peter was thinking at six in the morning when I wasn't there to listen. I've kept many of them. I wish I'd kept all of them. The thread that runs through them was that thing that his critics called sentimental, a romantic notion of the Canada he had in mind, the Canada of the North, Medicare, hockey, peace-making, human rights, Marshall McLuhan and snow. Here are some excerpts. All begin with "Patsy":

"At the heart of what's getting me down is that this country which has been for me not only the place I live but the subject of what I do for a living – my beat as sports has been Bill Frayne's or politics Peter Newman's – just seems to be slipping away. We can't handle Quebec. The Reform Party tells us what's happening in the West. All the institutions that help to define us – the trains, a national airline, a broadcasting network (whose television gets more American in style every year, even as its Canadian content grows), the social safety network (which *is* under attack) – are all in trouble."

"I'm not quite sure what the central question is, but I suspect it's somehow an attempt to see if the 'élite' are ahead of the people on a number of issues. My own guess is that a normally tolerant populace – well, for the most part tolerant – is fed up with being *told* to be tolerant. This is especially galling when the 'élite,' by which I mean politicians and the media, doesn't seem to be able to grapple with the *real* issues, jobs, crime, taxes, bureaucracies."

"I see 'Scrabble – 12 minutes' up on the board next week. Hour three, Monday. I think we're missing something. It's *very* widespread. In Inuvik, I learned that they're using it to teach literacy in the north. I'd really like to do a half hour with lots of angles. Isn't this just what we need to help fight the doldrums?"

"I think we should do something about Clayoquot Sound. Christ, it's now 813 people arrested. If it were Toronto . . ."

"I need to stand back from everything and say what is this country, what can it be? Where did it really come from, where is it going? Is it worth it?"

"This is written at 6 a.m. so I could be wrong."
He wasn't.

PATSY PEHLEMAN, *Toronto*

In 1997 when Peter Gzowski left CBC Radio's *Morningside* after fifteen years of hosting the show for a grinding three hours a day, five days a week, he took some of the country with him. Though the truth was not known publicly for a year or so, he departed because he was dying. A lifetime addiction to cigarettes and drink, particularly the former, had destroyed his health and the stress of even one more season would have been too much.

Eventually he quit both addictions, a triumph of will that came too late. His final years were an agony of humiliation and exhaustion, as emphysema smothered his lungs. He was attached permanently to an oxygen supply, which he had to trundle everywhere, and when venturing away from home he also needed a walker for support.

That sad ending isn't what Canadians will remember about Peter Gzowski. He won hearts across the land because he believed in this country's integrity, and his faith gave Canadians a sense of their own stature that somehow had begun to slip away. Everything he did in his public life proclaimed that this country stirred his heart, and consequently people everywhere were moved to appreciate the infinite acts of kindness that unite a community.

Gzowski's legacy rests upon the bedrock of good timing. He took over the CBC's flagship morning show in 1982 just as he and Canada were superbly ready for one another. What he offered on his side of the deal was his expertise gained as an eminent journalist and editor, where his great gift was an abundance of curiosity, without which journalists might far better choose careers as stuffed owls.

The country, for its part, was suffering from an extreme case of the blahs and desperately in need of an injection of confidence. The euphoria that gripped the land during the giddy success of Expo 67 had evaporated, leaving a hangover of grumpiness compounded by the conviction that Quebec would soon separate.

Gzowski would have none of it. He fell back on his years as a boy in Galt and editor on small-town newspapers who knew first-hand the common sense and ingenuity of people who live close to weather. He built his new show on the premise that exceptional villagers in one part of the country should know about exceptional villagers elsewhere in the country. What he proved, in short order, was that the country is jam-packed with exceptional people.

The content of *Morningside* seemed to emerge effortlessly from the fabric of a good land, but sophisticated machinery was grinding away in the basement. A team of the best producers and hot young researchers in radio created story ideas, located charming, articulate guests and prepared background material. Gzowski unfailingly gave them much credit, but his contribution was the inestimable one of mood. He had a genius for disarming guests, many of whom had never been on radio before. For one thing, the man so beloved by millions was a dishevelled disaster. His clothes, richly dappled with cigarette ash and pierced by burns, appeared to have been assembled from discards found in a bus shelter. His pale blue eyes, squinting behind serious spectacles, conveyed the comforting message that radio was no big deal and what was to follow would be fun. He was soon beloved by millions. No one expressed better what every Canadian wanted to *be* than Peter Gzowski.

Morningside was as eclectic as the man himself, and what mattered to Peter Gzowski came to matter to the whole country. A natural musician himself, he gravitated to Canadian musicians; because he cared about good writing, he brought on a parade of poets, and novelists, and regional celebrants; he loved Quebec, where he once struggled to learn French, so that province was in the loop; he was a political junkie. Most of all, he was passionate about the Canadian North, and astonished Canadians learned that a place called Iqaluit was something of a hub of activity.

Gzowski's noble efforts to eliminate adult illiteracy in Canada provide a textbook example of how one person can make a difference. Over the years he raised more than seven million dollars for that struggle, mostly from celebrity golf tournaments bearing his name.

He was a troubled person, for sure. The man known to the country for his unflappable good humour dealt with dark pieces of his nature, just like everyone else on the planet. Towards the end of *Morningside*, he began to dread the oblivion of departing the stage. He said to a friend, pretending it was a funny line, "I don't know who I'll be when I am no longer Peter Gzowski." He could have saved himself the anxiety. The truth is he'll always be the Peter Gzowski who pulled the country together, and gave Canadians back their best selves. His gift was handsomely presented and received everywhere with great love.

JUNE CALLWOOD, *Toronto*

When *Morningside* was to have the last show in Moose Jaw, the chance of getting tickets were slim. Several of us got together and said, well, if they are at the Spa there is a very nice park across the street. Why don't we go there so we will be near the action? Well, things progressed to a chartered bus and a pancake breakfast, as we had to be there for the beginning – seven a.m., I think. What really was great was that the CBC crew had set up some equipment so we could hear the broadcast as it was going live across Canada. People were very quiet as we all listened to that last *Morningside*. When the show ended, there were tears and a quietness and finally applause.

We climbed in the bus and went back to Regina just in time to hear *Morningside* as it got to CBC Saskatchewan. We listened to it amidst a large crowd at Victoria Park in downtown Regina. What a day!

CATHY ANDERSON, *Regina*

Much is made of Peter Gzowski's "gravelly" voice; many believe it was the secret of his success on radio. The voice certainly helped but then there have always been fine voices, "gravelly" or otherwise pleasing, on the airwaves, and few have had the magic of Gzowski's.

The first time I heard him on CBC Radio was in the midsixties. We had lost touch since university days, and suddenly there he was one evening narrating a documentary on the Beatles. And in his voice was that mischief, the barely suppressed laughter, almost a schoolboy giggle, that made working with him on the *Varsity* so much fun a decade earlier.

Laughter is tricky for a radio host; it can backfire. Laughter can make listeners uncomfortable; it can irritate them and, worst of all, it can patronize them. When Gzowski laughed the whole audience joined in. This is what people have remarked on so much since he died, this gift of his for talking to everyone the same way.

Radio is the perfect showcase, of course, for his sort of gift, but then radio is a wondrous medium in itself. Not because it reaches a mass audience. What makes radio special is that it speaks to each individual member of that audience as though he or she is the only one who matters. And as we all know that is a very endearing and reassuring quality.

When I lived in Russia in the early nineties, I used to plead with people there to speak English to me so I could put them on the radio in Canada as they really sounded. They worried about their bad grammar but it seemed to me that their very clumsiness meant they spoke from the heart. Like a young woman in Moscow talking about the collapse of the Soviet Union. What was it like to wake up one day to be told that everything she had been taught to value in her life was really worthless? She struggled for words and then she found them: "My heart is full of pain," she said.

In Moscow, one evening in 1993, we were fighting with the short-wave radio in the kitchen of our small apartment. Suddenly, in the midst of the crackling and distortion, a familiar voice said, "Holy cow!" And then he laughed and so did his guests, whoever they were. And then we lost the signal. But from half a world away, for the second it took him to say "Holy cow," we felt again the magic that Gzowski made on radio.

ELIZABETH GRAY, *Toronto*

It was an afternoon sometime during the first season of *Some of the Best Minds of Our Time*, and I was on the phone with Peter, he from home, me from the office at CBC. Peter, as always, was in efficient telephone communication mode – the briefer the exchange, the better. Nothing extraneous; just the facts. Perhaps it was the impatience in his voice that made me do it.

"Soooo," I began lazily, "whaddya have for lunch?" Long pause. "Sausages," he finally responded, bemused. I continued. "And how's the wife?" A burst of embarrassed laughter (his). "She's wonderful, as always. . . . How's yours?" He counter-challenged, ever the competitor. We were, after almost four years of working together, on completely uncharted territory. No previous conversation had veered even a millimetre beyond work, beyond the story, beyond the issue at hand. As we hung up, he was still chuckling uncomfortably, and I could picture him giving his head a rueful shake as his free hand (the one without the cigarette) sorted his bangs over to one side.

When I began working with Peter at *Morningside*, I was scared senseless. I was dealing with an icon and producing live radio. For my debut item, I neurotically fussed over minute details. I called the guest in Vancouver umpteen times to make sure everything was okay. I didn't sleep the night before.

On the appointed morning, I found myself hovering in the control room, as anxious as an expectant father pacing a maternity ward circa 1950. Leslie, the production assistant, got on the phone to the Vancouver studio. My guest hadn't arrived. Five minutes later, no guest. Ten minutes later, still no guest. Peter, busy on air, raised his eyebrows in concern as the missing-guest updates reached him via the computer screen. "Are you sure you told the guest five-thirty?" Marieke, the studio director, asked me in a voice simultaneously calm and alarmed. I hadn't. Overlooking the first rule of live national radio – beware of time zone changes – I'd asked the guest to be at the studio at eight-thirty, meaning eight-thirty Toronto time, forgetting he was three hours behind. Panicked by the thought of fifteen minutes of dead air, I phoned the poor unsuspecting guest at home, woke him from a deep sleep and prevailed upon him to do a live interview from his bed. I was mortified by my mistake, but Peter took it in stride. Albeit a bit groggy, the guest was good; so was the story, the script. To Peter, that's what mattered.

In fact, what I came to respect most about Peter (I'd already figured out that he was damn brilliant from years of listening to him) was how forgiving he was of his co-workers' mistakes, particularly because these mistakes made him, not the rest of us, look foolish in public. As long as our work was good, more often than not (way more often than not) he'd shrug his shoulders and let it go. And if we were going to mess up, best to mess up spectacularly, as Peter had the ability to revel in the sheer awfulness of a truly bad item. What he couldn't stand was mediocre failure.

Boy, he was sharp. Every item has at least one weak spot, something all producers try desperately to hide from hosts, usually under a barrage of additional background briefing of dubious relevance. A seasoned producer can get pretty good at wallpapering the holes. But within thirty seconds of receiving a script from me, Peter would look over his glasses, the ones so filthy you'd swear he rubbed Vaseline on them, fix me with a stare and ask the one question that pierced the heart of the weak spot. I couldn't get anything past him, and he loved proving it.

Even in the third and final season of *Best Minds*, after several decades of plying his trade, Peter before an interview was like a kid preparing for his first date. He was jittery, wound up, excited. He'd pepper me with questions. Peter never took his skills or charms for granted. He worked and worked and worked to achieve what you heard on air. But by the summer of 2000, the focus and intensity he poured into *Best Minds* interviews (we taped upwards of two hours per guest) were taking their toll. What you heard on tape was Peter still very much in command of his voice, although it was thinner, reedier. But when he emerged from studio after these interviews, he was a man literally but quietly gasping for air.

By this time, our telephone conversations, at least daily during the production period, had gotten decidedly longer and looser. Something had shifted in Peter; there was a softness, an openness I hadn't noticed before. After taping, after he'd had a chance to catch his breath, Peter would wander with me back to my office – a pigsty that made Peter look like a neat freak – slouch in my lopsided extra chair, put his now celebrated scrawny white ankles up on my desk and shoot the breeze. The goings-on of our spouses, his kids and grandkids, my step-daughter, all regularly made their way into our exchanges. It was only during this period that I discovered something new about Peter: He was a delicious, ribald, had-you-on-the-edge-of-your-seat storyteller. This was a revelation because around the office during *Morningside* days, Peter was talked out. Of course, on air he was much more loquacious, but his job was to elicit other people's stories, not spin his own yarns.

These post-taping chats were replaced, in the last year of his life, by luncheons served by him at his apartment (amazing what he could whip up with a telephone and a take-out menu). The first time Peter opened the door to me sporting a portable oxygen tank, I almost burst into tears. I'd had no warning. But the oxygen, I quickly realized, provided him with more energy. He almost bopped around the apartment. He wasn't gasping. He talked about plans to travel to the Arctic. He gave me career advice. Into our conversations crept vague acknowledgements of inner emotional lives.

I last talked to Peter about a week before he died. I was finalizing arrangements for yet another lunch, this one with two other former colleagues he hadn't seen in a long time. He was thrilled at the prospect of the old-time gathering. "Bye love," he said gently as we signed off. I went to my Day-Timer and scrawled *Lunch with Peter* in big block letters at the appropriate spot. Several mornings later when I picked up the phone and heard Gill's voice, I knew what was coming, but I wasn't prepared. You see, as Peter got weaker his appetite for life seemed stronger. I never could bring myself to cross out our lunch date in my Day-Timer. Yet I find myself carefully avoiding the page it's written on each time I have to flip through the book.

MEREDITH LEVINE, *Toronto*

Cooking on the radio with Peter Gzowski was like having the whole country in your kitchen. He always asked just the right questions so everyone listening could see, smell and taste what we were making. And he always cooked in the studio so listeners could hear the sounds of food – the popping of popcorn, the sizzle of potato pancakes in the pan or the hissing of the blow torch for crème brûlée. Peter loved food and loved to cook. He understood that food feeds the soul as well as the body and that it is an important part of people's lives.

In the fall of 1996, Peter asked me for help with a kitchen makeover. He wanted to rejuvenate his menus, to eat more healthfully and to cook more of the weekday meals so Gillian Howard, his life partner, didn't have to do them all. And then he wanted to report on all of this in his monthly column in *Canadian Living* magazine. Peter and I planned menus, went shopping, restocked his kitchen cupboards and cooked until he was confident and happy in the kitchen. Here is one of his favourite recipes we cooked together.

Roasted Vegetable Pasta Salad
Peter loved the idea of roasting vegetables. He would make a big batch at least once a week and use some on pasta, some as a side dish and some for salad. Gill told me they would often

add other vegetables and sometimes sauté ground veal in a little olive oil, add lemon and toss that with the vegetables, too.

    2 heads garlic
    8 plum tomatoes, cut into wedges
    2 red peppers, cut into chunks
    2 yellow peppers (if available), cut into chunks
    1 bulb fennel, trimmed, halved and cut into wedges
    2 long thin Asian eggplants, cut into chunks
    1 large onion, peeled and cut into wedges
    2 tbsp (25 mL) olive oil
    1 tbsp (15 mL) each chopped fresh rosemary and thyme (or
    1/2 tsp/2 mL each dried)
    1 lb (500 g) pasta (penne, preferably)

    Dressing:
    2 tbsp (25 mL) balsamic vinegar
    salt and pepper
    2 tbsp (25 mL) olive oil
    1/4 cup (50 mL) shredded fresh basil
    2 tbsp (25 mL) chopped fresh mint

1. Cut top 1/4 off the heads of garlic. Wrap in aluminum foil. Place tomatoes, peppers, fennel, eggplants and onions in a single layer on one or two baking sheets lined with parchment paper. Place the package of garlic on the baking sheet, too.
2. Drizzle vegetables lightly with olive oil and sprinkle with rosemary, thyme, salt and pepper. Roast in a 400°F (200°C) oven for 40 to 45 minutes, until vegetables are tender and brown.
3. Meanwhile, cook pasta in a large pot of boiling, salted water.

4. While pasta is cooking, make the dressing. Combine vinegar with salt and pepper and oil in a large serving bowl. Squeeze in roasted garlic. Add vegetables, pasta, basil and mint. Toss well and season with salt and pepper to taste. Makes 6 to 8 servings

BONNIE STERN, *Toronto*

Let me tell you about the time Peter Gzowski met *The Simpsons*. Actually, they were two of the human creators of the hit animated TV show, who'd come to Toronto to speak to college students. One of my jobs as a *Morningside* producer was to bring some of the odd artifacts of popular culture to Peter's studio, sit them down and watch what happened. With *The Simpsons* I figured we had the holy grail: American cultural icon, meet Canadian cultural icon. But in the end we had a meeting of oil and water.

It started at one of our daily story meetings. As usual, Peter was half sitting on, half sliding off, one of our mismatched couches, with his lunch and a stack of letters from people with stories that really mattered. I was about to pitch two guys who produced a cartoon show. Story meetings are like a courtroom: You have to come prepared, make direct and cogent arguments, know your *Morningside* precedents and politely await sentencing. Peter knew about *The Simpsons* but had never watched the show. We rarely put American entertainers on *Morningside* just because they happened to be visiting Canada, for the simple reason that they rarely had anything to say.

For my argument I went for a familiar vein, the Americanization of Canada. Here was a chance to slide cultural imperialism under the microscope, really zoom in on the Gen X fixation on irony and Canada's enduring lockstep with Yankee fashion. It was less a pitch, more a sketch for a hopeless Master's thesis. Peter knew that. He liked to deflate overblown ideas, gently (usually), not with a stab, but by peering over his glasses as if to say: Slow down, boy. Will it make good radio? Will they be funny? He sat up, elbows to knees, put his small carton of milk on the floor. This usually meant he was thinking of the right way to say something. Remember John Candy? he asked. John Candy had been on *Morningside* in the days of the Jarvis Street radio building, and we'd asked him to stick around after his interview and co-host the weekly report from Alberta with Peter. Neat idea, but on the radio as funny as a load of laundry. People who earn their livings making other people laugh sometimes opt not to do so when they're on their spare time. Peter knew his *Morningside* precedents better than anyone in the story-meeting courtroom. But he shrugged and said, Why not? and we moved on to the meatier matters in his stack of listener mail.

The Simpsons boys (pre-dot-com thirty-ish millionaires, one of them wearing a Daffy Duck tie) showed up on time and politely took their chairs in the studio with a man they'd never heard of before and presumably would forget as soon as they hit the Broadcast Centre's atrium after the interview. Peter worked his magic, or tried, looking for God in the details, where he knew He lived. Tell me about the parody of *H.M.S. Pinafore*; why *Pinafore*? Because it's in the public domain and doesn't cost us anything to use the music. Why this seeming fascination on *The Simpsons* with Canada, with CFL football and the Quebec referendum? Canada's funny. But why? It just is, the same way consonants are funny.

Another load of *Morningside* laundry. The same way consonants are funny? Our guests weren't used to this, a host who's curious and listens. They were used to Leeza Gibbons and *Entertainment Tonight*. Through the glass between the studio and control room, I got the over-the-glasses look. After a few more runs the boys warmed up, but that's as far as the interview ever went: tolerable, even somewhat comfortable, warm. We wouldn't grapple with Canada's slide into fifty-first statehood here. Peter knew that. We'd just chat with a couple of decent fellows who made a TV show. Don't have a cow, man.

They left, the show moved on, as always. There'd be another story meeting in a couple of hours.

Many shows, many story meetings and about three years later, Peter was in New York, to receive a Peabody Award, the broadcaster's equivalent of a Nobel Prize, a huge honour for him and the other recipients, who included the two co-creators of *The Simpsons*. Peter and *The Simpsons*, together again. Did you remember them, re-introduce yourself? I asked him when he came home.

Actually, he said, they remembered me.

TOM JOKINEN, *Toronto*

It was 1991 and I was a very young, very intimidated CBC producer sitting in on a *Morningside* story meeting.

I was a visitor from Regina, so I was an outsider in this élite group. My anxiety level spiked as the Great Man shuffled in.

He was in a rumpled, cigarette-flecked get-up that would shame a homeless person. I remember some especially ugly loafers – and no socks.

Patsy Pehleman, *Morningside*'s executive producer, introduced me to Peter. He said to me (very loudly!), "Oh, you're Prpick? You don't know how scared I was the first time I saw your name on a script!"

He was commenting on the unusual, consonant-rich spelling of my last name – a legacy of my Croatian heritage. My name is spelled P-R-P-I-C-K.

He told me – and all the other laughing producers in the room – that every time he saw my name on a script he was afraid he'd drop the second P and end up calling me "Sean Prick" on the air. Well, he never did. He always got it right, just like he always got "Saskatchewan" right.

Not "Saaa-skatch-oo-waaan," the way so many of his come-from-away colleagues said it on CBC Radio. He said it right: "Suh-skatch-uh-wun." But then he was from Saskatchewan. . . . Oh sure, he lived in the province for only eighteen months when he was a kid reporter for the Moose Jaw *Times-Herald*. But the two or three times I got to talk to him about his early professional life here, it was clear something "caught" him in Saskatchewan.

It would be pretty damn hard to find someone who loved this whole big, wide country as much as he did. But I believe Saskatchewan was in a special category of its own for him.

I suppose that's why he came here the last time I worked for him.

I was his advance man, working on the technical and logistical details of his *Morningside* finale in Moose Jaw in 1997.

I remember picking up this tired, drained, grey-looking old guy at the airport in Regina. He really looked awful. But after a quick scan of unlimited horizon off towards Moose Jaw – and a smoke – he seemed to gain strength and composure. And then we were off to do the show.

It was an intense couple of days, the most painful, wonderful, agonizing and rewarding days of my career, in fact. I remember Peter sending me to the Moose Jaw liquor store to buy him a bottle of Scotch. He thought people would be shocked and appalled if they saw him buying liquor, for God's sake! (I knew he'd probably get an ovation from the staff and customers the moment he walked in the door. But – what the hell! – I bought him the Scotch.)

I remember Peter and Stuart McLean screeching in laughter in a hotel room the night before the show as they ran through an absolutely ridiculous script involving a hissing cockroach.

I remember the crowd at the Temple Gardens Spa, visibly torn between joy at seeing their hero and sorrow at the fact they were there to say goodbye.

I remember (with sadness and irony now) as little old ladies came out of the crowd and tried to press smoking cures on him.

I remember the end of that final show as Peter stood slowly and painfully and tearfully for an ovation that lasted long, long after he signed off to the rest of Canada.

That was the defining moment of my life at the CBC, not because I did anything special, but just because I was there, within sight and earshot of history.

Peter, as I think back on those days and all the other days I got to work for you, I just want to say . . . thanks. Thanks for making the items I produced for you sing. Thank you for making me a better journalist by letting me know when I screwed up – and giving me personal and professional encouragement when I was wondering what the hell I was doing in this business.

And thanks for knitting my country together just a little bit tighter at a time when we really needed it.

You won't be forgotten and . . . better yet . . . somewhere, sometime, someone will build on your work to bring us – once again – a real Canadian radio show.

SEAN PRPICK, *Regina*

On Camera

In the fall of 1974, after just three seasons, Peter Gzowski walked away from *This Country in the Morning*, the most popular CBC radio program of its time. Gzowski and his executive producer, Alex Frame, were approached by Peter Herrndorf, then head of current affairs programming at CBC television. He was convinced that the team that had revolutionized morning radio could also revolutionize late-night television and in the process repatriate the Canadian late-night audience from Johnny Carson.

Those who have been heading to the Red Barn Theatre at Jackson's Point, Ontario, the first Monday in June for the past fifteen years or so to share an evening of Canadian writing, music and dance know for a certainty that Gzowski's unique blend of dry wit and boyish enthusiasm for great Canadian talent made for outstanding live theatre as well as great radio. Where else could you hear Ben Heppner belting out "Roll Over Beethoven" with the Barenaked Ladies? Herrndorf had been onto something.

I first met Gzowski in the spring of 1975 at CBC Television's current affairs production offices at 790 Bay Street in Toronto. Herrndorf's team had assembled a who's who of television producers and filmmakers from around the world, including the likes of Don Hewitt and Morely Safer from *60 Minutes* and Donn Alan Pennebaker, director of the classic cinema verité Bob Dylan documentary *Don't Look Back*, to instruct twelve of us in the art of making compelling television.

As the course was held in the months leading up to the launch of Herrndorf's first big project, *the fifth estate*, the majority were competing for slots on the new current affairs flagship, to be run by executive producer Glenn Sarty, who had been Adrienne Clarkson's exec on *Take 30* and on the two prime-time predecessors to *the fifth estate*, *Take 60* and *Adrienne at Large*. Clearly the two subversives taking the course were Alex Frame and Peter Gzowski, who were soaking up Television 101 in preparation for the launch of *90 Minutes Live*, Herrndorf's second big project.

The graduating assignment was to be a film suitable for airing on the current affairs prime-time flagship. No resources were spared and expectations were high. The finished products were unrelievedly earnest and forgettable, the one exception being the Gzowski-Frame submission, which was brilliant and unusable.

Without a hint of mischief, Gzowski was dispatched to the Toronto Beaches to conduct a rare interview with a famous collector of dog breath. Conducted on a park bench in the leafy green space along the boardwalk, the interview featured a close look at the eminent collector's scrapbook, complete with sealed baggies for each specimen, carefully labelled, identified by breed, age, collection date and location. The highlight of the piece was an exciting opportunity to see the collector's technique in action, racing along the boardwalk attempting to bag a sample or two with the help of startled and not always co-operative dog walkers.

Gzowski could be brilliant on television. Ten years after Television 101, Sarty asked Gzowski to host an interview show that was to be produced in every region of the country. Gzowski agreed only when Sarty promised no make-up and no make-over. While the *fifth estate* crew had been eager to pursue stories from the four corners of the planet, Gzowski was genuinely thrilled to go to Truro, Nova Scotia, to interview playwright John Gray; Consort, Alberta, to interview k.d. lang's mother; and Winnipeg, Manitoba, to attempt a pas-de-deux with Evelyn Hart. The resulting show, *Gzowski & Company*, made excellent television, with a comfortably rumpled Gzowski engaged in compelling conversation with fascinating Canadians. It was greeted with rave reviews.

For all that, radio was Gzowski's natural medium. He would say that when people watched him on television, they would comment on what he was wearing. When they listened to him on radio, they would comment on what was said.

Gzowski brought a writerly approach to what was essentially a performance medium. His tentative, roundabout, oblique way of approaching exactly the right question had the feel of a guy alone at a typewriter with his own thoughts, working out what it was he was trying to get at. Gzowski made us all feel better about ourselves because it is very hard work to be that present in the moment, as he would say, "to think fast and talk slowly," to ask what you would like to ask. Not to think of it later that day.

Gzowski was uncomfortable with the performance aspect of broadcasting. In our 1975 course he asked Patrick Watson, "When does art become artifice, when do you become a performer?" In his 1997 introduction to *The Morningside Years* he wrote that W.O. Mitchell had "snorted in derision when I insisted one evening that what I did on radio wasn't a performance (he was right of course . . .)."

His public persona, his artless voice, was of course a brilliant construction. I do not mean that cynically. I mean that with great affection and admiration for the professional discipline to be so self-aware, to come to the core of what made his conversations so successful, so compelling to others.

It also helped that his enthusiasms, his interests seemed to mirror my own. . . . How many millions across the country felt the same? Peter did not seem to have the sense that people's interests split into discrete boxes. Music, books, ideas, politics, economics, the news of the day were all of a piece to Peter. What's interesting? What are people talking about today? What can I bring to people to get them talking? It has surprised me, and it shouldn't have, to hear so many others repeat what I used to say about Gzowski . . . that I would often stop my car at the top of the ramp into our underground parking garage at work to hear the conclusion to some item that had me riveted.

DOUGLAS KNIGHT, *Toronto*

The first person ever to interview me was Peter Gzowski. The experience came close to finishing both of us. The early 1970s, it was. I was a brand-new writer then. My second book had just been published and happened to be chosen by the American Library Association as a Best Book for Young Adults. That got it reviewed in places that would ordinarily have ignored it, and one day the CBC phoned and asked if I'd care to be interviewed by Peter Gzowski. I was as new a landed immigrant as I was a writer. But even tourists knew Mr. Gzowski was the Voice of Canada – in Charlie Farquharson's memorable phrase, he was the only thing that united us all besides hatred of Air Canada coffee.

I hung up, told my wife the news and wandered around the house preening. Then I began to get really scared. Fortunately, one of the most respected writers in my field, Frederik Pohl, had just published an essay on what the young science-fiction writer needs to know about media interviews. Your greatest fear going in, Mr. Pohl wrote, is that you'll be caught with nothing to say. You think you should memorize amusing anecdotes, profound insights and trenchant quotes. Relax, he advised. The interviewer is a professional, experienced at coaxing interesting conversation from far duller people than yourself; you're far more likely to be left with urgent things unsaid.

I reached the studio reasonably confident. I had been told that this was to be television, rather than radio. I'd heard Peter had been given a show of his own, and I thought it a ducky idea – all of us were curious to know what he looked like. But I did not own a television (not too hip; too poor), so I'd never seen the show. Or Peter. I kept trying to spot him backstage, but kept getting distracted by some lunatic speed freak who'd slipped past security somehow and was pinballing around the entire area. Hunter S. Thompson would have considered this guy dangerously wired; he sprayed sweat and incomprehensible gibberish in all directions, and didn't seem to know he had two cigarettes going at once.

Finally, someone took him aside and murmured to him. He fixed his twitching eye on me . . . and to my horror, sprinted right up to me. And said, in an Alvin and the Chipmunks voice, perhaps the only words he could possibly have said that I would have grasped just then: "I liked your book." I couldn't believe it was him. On radio he was relaxed, mellow and easygoing. This guy was a poster boy for Tourette's syndrome. I began to sweat myself.

"So, Mr. Gzowski," I said, "now you've tried both, which do you prefer, television or radio?" I can quote his response: "Radio radio radio radio radio, definitely radio. Yes, radio."

I made one more try. "So . . . when will this air, do you know?" He stared at me. "We're live," he said finally. Now we were both crazed with fear.

The next thing I knew we were on camera, and the show was in progress. And Peter underwent the most astonishing transformation. Suddenly, he was the Peter Gzowski we all knew: calm, urbane, wise, gently witty. The first few questions were easy serves, and we got a few volleys going. I began to enjoy myself. And then . . . I've forgotten exactly what the question was. It was a very good question; that was the trouble. One of those profound questions that opens up many issues. For a moment, I froze. Then I remembered – I was in the hands of a pro. Thank God!

"Peter," I confessed, "I'm not smart enough to answer that in less than half an hour. You'd better ask me your next question." He froze. We grinned silently at each other, for an interval that may be called accurately either fifteen seconds of dead air or a million years of horror and shame.

Finally, somebody got the next question up on his screen, the interview lurched back into motion, and somehow we got through it without chewing open the veins in our wrists.

A year later, *90 Minutes Live* wasn't any more. Peter phoned, apologized for the fiasco, and asked me to be on his radio show. I accepted at once . . . and wondered if I'd made another mistake, because this, too, was going to be live, coast to coast.

The moment I entered the booth, I relaxed completely. He was sprawled in a comfortable chair, with his feet up on a console. He wore a wrinkled white T-shirt, sweatpants and slippers. He hadn't combed his hair that day. He looked genuinely happy to be alive, and there, and talking to me.

It didn't feel like an interview. It felt like a chance meeting with an old friend. I didn't notice when the red light went out, and neither did he; someone had to come and drag me out of the booth.

A few years after that, someone finally had the sense to give him a TV show that was not live, *Gzowski & Company*. He came to my home in Halifax, spent a whole day talking with me and my wife, Jeanne, about her company, Nova Dance Theatre, and our collaborative novel, *Stardance* – and with our eight-year-old about what it was like having artists for parents – and then he distilled all that tape down to a half hour that remains the best coverage Jeanne or I have ever had. They say you never forget your first time. I certainly never have.

SPIDER ROBINSON, *Bowen Island, British Columbia*

The most vivid encounter I had with Peter Gzowski was not on radio. It was during his purgatory with *90 Minutes Live*, the attempt – perhaps before its time, certainly before Peter was really fit for it – to build a late-night talk show in Canada. The panel that night included (a) a klatch from *Monty Python's Flying Circus*, who came on in women's clothes, and one of whom was in that state of advanced ossification best known as ape drunk; (b) a professional impersonator of the Queen, who, in contradistinction to the real Queen, acted imperiously when in role or out (I remember her ordering a taxi when the ordeal was over, with the tone of voice that suggested execution for the publicist should a taxi not appear – soon; she was not so much an impersonation as someone possessed); (c) the Duke of Ook (I am not making this up), a "pianist" – the scare quotes are emphatically necessary – who strode to a studio piano, hit a few discords, and then jumped up and down in the manner of an ape while furiously scratching his armpits; and (d) me.

This tea party took place in St. John's, which explains my presence in the conclave of horror and madness. It was a novel experience for me, being the only person on a panel that could even pretend to normalcy. My anxieties of having to navigate this witches' brew of live television were trivial compared to Peter's. After all, he was the host. He had to endure them all, for ninety minutes, in front of a studio audience and while being beamed to a fascinated, I suspect mesmerized and maybe even fearful, Canadian public.

This was not an occasion that geniality could save. It may seem now just a trifle ungracious to offer the anecdote when the themes of Peter's life and work are being, as they should be, rehearsed with gratitude and fondness by the very man whom he genuinely touched, and by whom he was much admired.

Well, he did endure. What is more, insofar as such a congeries of misfits and neurotics – myself included – could be held at bay, he did. It was a moment not of great polish but of admirable valour. It reminded me that Peter, besides the other virtues for which he is now being celebrated, had a performer's fortitude.

His real presence, of course, was through and on CBC Radio. And in that avatar, Peter was singularly in his element. The tone and fact of public broadcasting received its key signature from this one performer over the life of his career at the CBC. He was a friendly champion – if this adjective doesn't quite nullify that noun – of a certain idea of Canadianism. His career and inclination led him to the study of this country as a country.

It will be remembered that his first major program was called *This Country in the Morning*. His taste and evangelism on behalf of Canadian letters was always part of a fuller campaign to find the best and most distinctive of Canada, give it notice and celebration.

He had an in-studio presence that was formidable, a beguiling quality – both of voice and manner – that hid a deep earnestness with the job at hand. He worked to prepare, he had goals when he set out to talk to someone, and he was professional in the way we say musicians or actors are professional – they labour to acquire skills that they equally labour to conceal.

His connection with what may be fairly called the CBC constituency was deep and intense. It is remarkable what his three-hour stints each morning achieved over time. His voice, the subjects he (with others) chose, the emphases he gave to certain ideas and people constituted a soft agenda for a type of Canadian pride.

I think this was all to the good. We Canadians are too loose in our apprehension of this country. We too infrequently take the inventory of what we are, who we are and why we matter. Peter Gzowski was a goad to Canadians' complacency about their country, and a genuine, necessary and intelligent booster of this country's virtues.

Add to that, he was a zealous friend to Canadian letters, and to the men and women – academics, novelists, essayists and publishers – who hold Canadian letters in their care. He had that fundamental insight that the arts, broadly understood, are the nurture of a citizenry, and he as a national host (in his case, that term has a double ring) was there to introduce, diffuse and praise the arts of the country to the country.

This is, was, a large consignment for any career. When I saw him last, he was still at it, in his capacity as chancellor of Trent University. This was a large, skilful, serious man, an example to anyone in the broadcast profession, and a very jewel to those who care about Canada.

REX MURPHY, *Toronto*

This is the true story, as I remember it, of Peter Gzowski and Nancy Mickleburgh, Beaver Lady of New Brunswick. I had the pleasure of working on *90 Minutes Live*, that brave, experimental and, okay, ultimately ill-fated late-night television program. Those of us who lived it, however, remember only its camaraderie and its many hilarious, shining moments.

One of these occurred during a week of special programming from Halifax. As producers, we were always looking for new ways to amuse and entertain our host, who had a low boredom threshold. Nancy Mickleburgh, in her late seventies, hadn't invented wheels, nor had she won people's votes, but she'd be a Halifax guest along with auto designer Malcolm Bricklin, politician Flora MacDonald and the Men of the Deeps. What Nancy *had* done was remarkable: She had tamed beavers in the wild.

On the phone, she was a plainspoken conservationist who claimed to be "better than Grey Owl." Owl, according to her, was a phoney; she was the real thing. She didn't live with a bunch of tame beavers in the house. No, sir. Her beavers were wild, unspoiled. Well, perhaps a little spoiled. They lived in their natural habitat but swam to her for carrots when she shouted their names.

She'd named her beavers after movie stars and politicians. There was Pierre Elliott Trudeau beaver and Marilyn Monroe beaver. We couldn't resist going to film her. We (me, the sound man and the cameraman) drove down remote rural roads to get to Nancy's place. It was a freezing cold morning. Finally, the house. Behind, down a hill, the pond. Within barking distance, fifty metres away, a beaver dam. Problem: The water downstream was frozen solid. We got axes and started breaking ice. "This one's for Pete," we shouted, chopping away.

Eventually, after thoroughly interfering with Mother Nature, we got what we came for: great footage of a dedicated, determined old woman standing at water's edge calling beavers like children. Her voice was wavery but inviting. Two valiant beavers finally took the splash off the dam, then hove into view, plugging away through the ice chips, then we watched them drag their definitely-not-house-trained, sleek bodies out of the water and take carrots from Nancy's hand.

Peter didn't see the film until it was rolled into the show. Nancy was on the set, looking pleased. Secretly, she had decided to honour Peter by naming a new beaver after him. Peter Gzowski beaver was too shy to appear, but we had Nancy on film, bellowing his name into the wind.

Peter cracked up. What could be more Canadian, after all, than having a beaver named after you?

ANNE BAYIN, *Toronto*

Television had given Peter Gzowski a hard time the first time out. His 1970s late-night talk show was reviled by audiences and critics alike. *90 Minutes Live*, like so many of the CBC's attempts to create its own night-time talk-show franchise, was an unmitigated flop. So when Tapestry Pictures was preparing to launch *Gzowski in Conversation*, Peter's return to the CBC television network in 1999, we wanted to do it right. Right for the audience and, most important, right for Peter. By now, after years of radio, Peter Gzowski's household reputation had reached Herculean proportions, and I felt like a crusader with the biggest grail imaginable. We worked closely with Peter and with CBC's Slawko Klymkiw to design a format that made entertainment and intellectual sense. We hired segment producers Peter knew and trusted. Producers with depth and humour and a sense of Peter's interview style. We designed an original set, jokingly referred to as Possum Lodge, filled with paintings and sculptures by contemporary Canadian artists whose work he loved. Tables and chairs were warm wood and woven fabrics with no glass or brass in sight. We assembled an exceptional, talented crew who among other things were die-hard *Morningside* devotees. And we found two remarkably special women, Joan Tosoni, our warm and witty director, whom Peter first met on the East Coast Music Awards, and wardrobe designer Trysha Bakker.

Fashion isn't the first thing one thinks of when one thinks of Peter Gzowski. Unless, that is, you're the executive producer with a cantankerous star bent on wearing his own threadbare slacks and slumpy sweaters with more pills than Liza Minelli. If pressed to describe Peter's personal style, I'd have to say comfy, with a touch of the Mad Trapper, liberally sprinkled with rubbed-in cigarette ash and coffee stains. But this was national television and we knew Peter would ultimately be much happier if he felt he looked presentable on camera. Enter Trysha Bakker. Trysh made her mark in the world of film and television dressing the likes of Robert Mitchum, Bernadette Peters and Rob Lowe. Not the first person who pops to mind for wardrobe consultant to our star. But born and raised in the Ottawa Valley, Trysha grew up on a diet of *Morningside*, Can Lit and a deep love of real people. Her years with Hollywood's finest had, if anything, made her distaste for pretension ever more acute. And her bathroom humour got many reluctant celebrities over their nerves. For Peter and Trysha it was love at first sight.

By the time I arrived at Harry Rosen's flagship showroom Peter and Trysha were old buddies, laughing at what was no doubt one of Trysha's raunchy inseam quips. Rosen's staffer Bob Denham had been selected by Trysh, and a private dressing room in the inner sanctum of Harry's had been turned into Peter's star dressing room. He was working hard to be co-operative but the whole thing was definitely not Peter's style. The fruit and flowers we had carefully placed for his pleasure were pushed aside for Peter's rumpled copy of the morning papers, a Styrofoam cup of cold coffee and the ever-present ashtray. And, to his mortification, I had arrived to oversee the fashion show. As Peter grumped and struggled with belts and buttons, I was trying to think of all the jobs each outfit would have to do: a casual look for the Comics, the Actors, the Violin; an urban, upscale image for Diana Krall and Christopher Plummer; a cleaned-up version of comfy and rumpled, vintage Peter, for Jann Arden, Murray McLauchlan and Doris McCarthy; unpretentious and understated for his old friends Farley Mowat and Wayne Gretzky; and a proper Bay Street grey suit for Conrad Black. I was there to select. Peter was there to model.

This was Peter Gzowski, an icon to my generation and a man whose character and intelligence I secretly revered. I not only wanted his respect but I wanted to deliver to him the television audience he deserved, his loyal fans who were clamouring for more of him. I knew that to do that I, in turn, would have to do things he may not at first think had any value whatsoever. Like clothes.

It was the Zegna jacket that got him. Sure, the slacks were perfectly cut and comfortable and made him look, well, classy. The shirts Trysha and Bob had found were his colour, his size, his cut and, well, classy. The shoes all fit. The ties were quiet, yet stylish. But it was the jacket that got him. It was tweed, browns with a shot of blue thread. Warm, soft, perfectly cut. And it fit like a dream. When I think of it now, it was a moment I know I will never forget. He had grumbled and grumped. He had rejected a lot of stuff out of hand. And he had very reluc-tantly shambled into the anteroom a couple of times to give me a look at a few sweaters. But when he slipped his arms into that jacket, held by quiet Bob, and even as Trysha tugged at the hem and adjusted the shoulders, you could see the corners of Peter's mouth edging into a smile. He looked at the front view, he shrugged a couple of times getting it to sit just right, then, right in front of my eyes, Peter Gzowski did a perfect 360-degree pirouette! I tried to contain my delight. He likes it! Maybe this was going to work after all.

Postscript: *Gzowski in Conversation*, designed as a weekly prime-time show, was never scheduled in that slot. The show ran on CBC Newsworld and eventually on CBC Network as a daytime summer replacement. Viewers, when they could find it, loved it. Critics grudgingly admitted Gzowski had found his place on television. But CBC quietly let the franchise drift away, and after two unforgettable seasons of now legendary interviews and performances by many of Canada's truly great, *Gzowski in Conversation* joined his other television forays in the Gzowski lore and legend.

MARY YOUNG LECKIE, *Toronto*

There are two things I know about Peter Gzowski. One, he gave me my first break. And two, he would do anything for his children.

I know these things because the first time I was a guest on *Morningside* had very little to do with the fact that I had written a play and everything to do with the fact that his daughter Alison, who was living in Newfoundland at the time, told her father he had to interview me and give me my break. No ifs, ands or buts.

The problem, I imagine, with being Peter Gzowski was interviewing people like me for the first time. I spent the entire ten minutes of the interview thinking, "Wow, I can't believe I'm being interviewed by Peter Gzowski." I was so in awe of the guy that I forgot to answer any of the questions. But we got through it, and Peter pulled off the impossible. He made it sound like I knew what I was talking about, which I didn't.

He did a big favour for me that day, and over the next twelve years or so that was pretty much our relationship. Peter never stopped doing me favours and giving me breaks.

It wasn't a unique relationship. There are hundreds of actors and musicians and writers across Canada he did this for. Once Peter was in your corner – and he was in a lot of corners – he would do anything to help you. And more often than not, he would help in ways that went far beyond what anyone could describe as the duties of a radio host.

I sent Peter a script once, and he recorded his voice and allowed me to use it in a play. He was playing himself, on radio, and poking fun at himself, night after night, in theatres all over the country. He came on 22 *Minutes* and poked fun at himself – twice. He came on *Made In Canada* and poked fun at himself. He wrote the foreword to a book I released, and although he didn't make fun of himself, it could have easily ruined his reputation as a guy who knew good writing when he saw it. I knew full well that having "Foreword by Peter Gzowski" on the cover meant more sales than I ever would have had alone; when I thanked him for the introduction, he told me he was happy to do it, that in fact the book was almost as good as he said it was in the introduction.

It's hard to pick a Gzowski moment that is appropriate for a collection such as this. It's tempting to try to sum up the way Canadians felt about him. But Alison's advice – and Alison is her father's daughter – was to share not an appropriate

Gzowski moment but rather a favourite one. My favourite moment with Gzowski was the time we spent together in jail. Peter was in Halifax on a book tour. And being Peter, he agreed to appear on 22 *Minutes* and do a bit with me. My idea was that instead of a quick interview we would do a sketch together.

The idea was that I would approach Peter at his book signing and ask to discuss what it means to be a Canadian. Peter, in his Mr. Canada persona, would suggest that we get together afterwards and have a discussion about Canada over "a nice cup of tea." Then we'd cut to the two of us in a crazy bar, drinking whisky, and I'd say, "I thought you said we were having a cup of tea," and Peter would say, "This is my cup of tea." Then we'd hit the town; we'd go to a pile of bars and get in all sorts of trouble, make it up as we went along and video-tape the entire thing.

Peter thought this was my best idea yet. The next hurdle was Peter's very capable assistant, Shelley. Shelley called me and asked me exactly how many bars we would be visiting. I told her about four, omitting to mention that it being Halifax, each of the four bars had at least three bars inside the bar. She asked me what we would be drinking. I assured her that this was TV, and on TV, when people drink, they never really drink, they drink apple juice. On TV people don't *get* drunk, they *act* drunk. "After all," I pointed out, "we are a very professional show. We're on the CBC, for God's sakes."

She made me repeat it. Apple juice. Acting.

The very first bar we went to had a punk band on stage. The room was packed with kids with green hair and shaved heads and pierced faces. And there was Gzowski, surrounded by people with rings in their noses and chains running from their ears to their eyebrows, and they were talking to him like he was a rock star.

That's the way it was with Peter. His demographic included Nan who would never miss a book signing and it included the girl with the blue hair who wanted him to sign her jacket with her eye shadow.

So we got ready to shoot, we saddled up to the bar, and I told the bartender, "We're going to have apple juice." And the bartender said, "Apple juice?" I said, "Well, it's TV, on TV you drink apple juice." And Peter, who as we all know never really had much time for the constraints of television, looked at me and said, "We're not really drinking apple juice in front of this crowd, are we?"

They say one of the hardest things to do, as an actor, is to pretend you're getting progressively drunk as the night goes on. Peter and I gave excellent performances that night. We shot at all the bars; we stayed up very late. We went to a tattoo parlour; we stood on a street corner and yelled at the moon. Which is when the cops showed up. Which you have to admit is a pretty good ending, so I asked them would they do us a favour and take us in. As a rule police officers are notoriously shy about appearing on television in uniform. But the officers had one look at the two of us and informed us it would be an honour to lock Mr. Gzowski up.

The night ended with us sitting in a jail cell in Dartmouth with the door locked. Fade to black.

Even though it had been ten years since that first radio interview, when the camera stopped rolling and we were sitting there waiting for someone to let us out, all I could think was, "Wow, I can't believe I'm in jail with Peter Gzowski."

And Peter looked around and said, "I like this town."

Now that's a great Canadian.

RICK MERCER, *Halifax*

Peter Gzowski's Canada

There was a time when I thought Canada was being held together by Peter Gzowski and blind hope.

— *ANNA FRASER, Eureka, Nova Scotia*

Your voice will for me always be associated with the smell of coffee and bacon cooking on the wood stove, and all things Canadian.

— *DEAN WHITING, via e-mail*

It was three hours earlier in Hollywood than back East, and the post-Oscar parties had gone on until the wee hours of the morning, so I was pretty groggy when Peter Gzowski called my hotel room with congratulations on my Academy Award win for the documentary *If You Love This Planet*.

Later in the day some friends phoned wanting to hear all about the ceremony and parties and the movie stars I'd met, and one of them said, "So what was *the* most exciting thing that happened?"

I blurted, "Peter Gzowski called!"

You see, it was as if my country had called. For me, Peter personified Canada, and his call felt like the embrace of an entire nation. It was Peter. My country had called.

But then again, my friends were Canadian, so there was no need to explain.

TERRE NASH, *Montreal*

When I was a child, Peter took me to all the parts of Canada I couldn't afford to visit. He invited me to think about what I believed and explore ideas with others as I journeyed through university. Many times, a discussion would spark an idea for the beginning of a political science or sociology paper and provide me with an extensive list of resources for my research. Years later, I sat at my convocation. I was prepared for a long and boring presentation. You cannot imagine the joy in my heart when I read the program – Keynote Address: Peter Gzowski. He gave an incredible address that left me with a vision of Canada and the world I was about to discover. I stopped and shook his hand after I received my degree and floated off the stage. I couldn't have been happier.

MARTINA PAYETTE, *Airdrie, Alberta*

Peter Gzowski proved that you didn't have to be famous to be fascinating. There was always hope that some day my phone would ring and a *Morningside* producer would want me on the show to talk about that excellent paper I submitted at school or my funky hat collection.

Peter, you made me laugh, think and cry. You showed me that all people have a great story to tell, and that Canada is a wonderful place to be.

EMILY CAMPBELL, *Regina*

Professor Gzowski, My name is Sean. I met you for the first time when I was a rebel-rousing nineteen-year-old back in 1989. You might say I was a somewhat wayward child interested in instant gratification and little else. Drinking or another method of getting high was limiting my world. However, during a stint as a construction labourer, despite my wishes, the CBC was always drumming away in the background. In short, I started listening to you, Peter, and never stopped. My horizons were gradually broadened, and my life enriched and changed forever. You began my education in life, love and language prior to my traditional university education. Thank you, Professor Gzowski. There is a part of you in me and all Canadians.

Therefore I will raise a glass to you this evening, because you showed me how.

SEAN MALBY, *Toronto*

On one of his shows, Peter spoke admiringly about his William Baffin Explorer roses. Of course, I went out and bought two of these roses, which are now at least ten feet tall. Each year they have an abundance of flowers.

All Explorer roses are named after Canadian explorers. I was thinking I'd love to buy an Explorer rose named Peter Gzowski. It would be a small tribute to a great man who explored this country and then guided *Morningside* listeners on journeys so that they, too, could see its beauty.

KATHRYN DAVIES, *Newmarket, Ontario*

Because Peter was always there (I first heard him on *This Country in the Morning* when I was a kid in New Brunswick), I made the mistake of assuming that he always would be there. I wrote to him and told him about my life – personal things that he was gracious enough to seem interested in. He once took a two-dollar bill signed by my mum all the way with him to Victoria, where it was signed by my brother-in-law; in Calgary Peter signed it then gave it to me – a quintessential Canadian thing, the two-dollar bill and the scattered family, eh?

After my twin daughters were diagnosed with CF, I felt like the stuffing was knocked out of me and I sort of lost the ability to write about these things, although I *thought* letters to Peter quite often – kind of therapy to help me organize things in my head, I guess.

My dad was in the army, and I grew up an army brat. Everywhere Dad was posted, my mum and dad would take us – my sisters and me – to see all kinds of places they'd read about, so we got to see a lot of Canada. By the time I was ten years old, I'd been to every province except Newfoundland (I got there when I was nineteen). I never felt like any particular place in Canada was home – it *all* was. My parents gave me Canada by letting me benefit from their curiosity.

When I moved to Medicine Hat (for keeps, it now looks like, after twenty-three years) I didn't see much of Canada any more. Circumstances like health and money interfered. Then Peter Gzowski and *Morningside* gave Canada back to me. To hear from all parts of the country, many of which I'd lived in or visited, was wonderful. Thanks to Peter's curiosity and his skilled colleagues on the show, Canadians got to see themselves – places, issues, arts . . . everything. And, no matter what people say about Gzowski's *illusion* of Canada as a bunch of small towns, this was certainly the Canada I had lived in. Even in Edmonton I had lived not in a huge city but in a small neighbourhood. So, from the bald-ass prairie – thanks, Peter, for delivering to us Ucluelet, BC, Pond Inlet NWT, Hinton AB,

Eyebrow Sask., Portage La Prairie MN, Havelock ON, Saint-Jean-Chrysostome PQ, Jemseg NB, New Dominion PEI, West Jeddore NS, and Pouch Cove Nfld. I'll miss you.

KRISTA MUNROE, *Medicine Hat, Alberta*

I immigrated to Canada in 1989 from the United States. Peter Gzowski taught me the richness of Canadian life – of what it means to be a Canadian. I became a citizen as soon as possible, and I remember when I took my test. I had prepared diligently but blew a question about the second-largest producer of lumber in Canada. I had been totally prepared to hum the *Morningside* theme – I thought that would have been a more important question.

LOIS ADDISON, *Dunrobin, Ontario*

During my working years I was able to listen to *Morningside* only when driving to a meeting out of town. One of the most distant trips was a drive from Whitehorse to Inuvik. The observatory in Inuvik needed an upgrade and there was a week's work. I wanted to see some of the wilderness close at hand; I had demonstrated to my boss that a return flight to Whitehorse plus car rental was cheaper than flying the whole way; and I volunteered to travel on weekends.

I was well past Eagle Plains, the only vestige of civilization on the way, and feeling, well, isolated in the wilderness, when I tuned into a weak CBC station, and there was the familiar Gzowski voice reminding me that I was still in Canada, a reassurance that all was well. This is Canada, eh?

JOHN FIRTH, *Ottawa*

My siblings and I are CBC junkies. I finally recognized the seriousness of my addiction a few years ago when I needed some reference forms completed to ascertain my fitness for a management position. Part of the reference went something like this: "The candidate most often begins sentences with . . ." followed by four clauses of varying confidence.

One of my good friends called and said, "Laurie, I can't do this. There is no option that says, 'This morning on Gzowski I heard . . .'."

LAURIE STEPHENSON, *Head of Saint Mary's Bay, Nova Scotia*

I never knew him but I knew him well; I never met him but I met him often.

I came to Canada in 1974 from Scotland and I learned more about this country from him than from anybody else I've met in twenty-seven years.

BILL McLEAN, *London, Ontario*

In 1998, I went to The Seeing Eye, in Morristown, New Jersey (USA), to receive and be trained with my first guide dog. Although I had travelled abroad in my youth to visit family, this was my first time completely alone in a foreign country. Obviously, I missed my family, but I also missed Canada.

I spent considerable time thinking about this, in order to find exactly what it was about Canada that I missed. What Canadian icon, artist, place would symbolize Canada best? Then, one day, as I was walking to my room after dinner, the theme from *Morningside* popped into my mind, for no particular reason that I could discern. What I was missing during my time in New Jersey was that truly Canadian essence that Peter Gzowski brought to our consciousness.

ADELE FAROUGH, *Ottawa*

I spent many years travelling the roads of Saskatchewan with Peter Gzowski as my only constant companion in the morning. His thoughtful literate style and always fresh enthusiasm for life kept me going on days when not much else seemed of interest.

Although I have lived in almost every part of our great country, Peter constantly showed me new and wondrous people and places.

They say a person never truly dies as long as there is one person who remembers him with love. If that is the case, then through friends he may not have ever met, Peter Gzowski should live darn near forever.

MICHAEL MYERS, *Regina*

What was it? His voice? His demeanour? Candour? The little stammer? It was all those things and more that drew me in and made me feel that I was part of something very special. And then the program would end and I would feel alone.

OWEN McDERMOTT, *via e-mail*

In many ways, Canada could be seen as an impractical nation with its long distances, diverse citizens and the strong influence of our neighbour to the south. How could anyone bring together a country like this? I doubt that our politicians have it figured out, but I know that Peter Gzowski did.

BARBARA CAMPBELL, *Palgrave, Ontario*

The man was a paradox to me. There was no one like him, and yet he was like all of us. He knew more about everything than I did, but the questions that bedevilled him were the same ones that kept me awake at night. He was no angel, but somehow the times he was most cantankerous were the times that endeared him to us the most. He hated being cast as hero, and that just made him more heroic in our eyes.

Maybe someday, when I look up "Canadian" in the dictionary, I'll find his picture there. That would be fine by me.

JACK VANDER HOEK, *Ottawa*

My neighbour spends a lot of time on a tractor and was introduced to Gzowski in 1996, only a year before he left the air. My neighbour was disappointed when he left *Morningside*. He said, "I was just getting to know him and now he's gone." Well, it seems that whether you knew him for a long time or only a moment, he left his mark. I imagine his words rolling across my fields and continuing across this great country forever.

MARK WILSON, *New Liskeard, Ontario*

I moved to Canada as a teenager with my family from Britain. My introduction to Canada came through my Grade 11

classroom in Niagara Falls, Ontario. Culturally, ideologically
and socially I did not fit. I found my classmates and teachers
unwilling to tolerate my differences. Nor were they willing to
share their Canada with me. I was an unwanted alien. Canadian
people appeared to be as cold and heartless as the bleakest
winter day.

And then I heard Peter. He projected a Canada that was
completely different. He opened doors that showed the full
wonder of this great country, the treasure of its diversity and
the wealth that is not only the existence of differing points of
view and experiences, but a wealth that comes from embracing
and encouraging us to experience those differences.

Peter showed me the Canada I wanted to live in.

CRAIG WILSON, *via e-mail*

I have been trying to put into words what Peter did for us. The
best I can come up with is this: Peter led a talking circle for this
whole, huge country. He made neighbours of us all.

It is not easy to keep Canada together, nor is it easy to
always be both rational and compassionate towards our
Quebec neighbours. It was interesting to hear the comments
from Quebec about Peter. I want to say this: Even if many in
Quebec could not care less, Peter helped us to care about
them. I was a better person, even in a day-to-day way, because
of Peter. He did not just *reflect* our better selves; he opened us
up to be genuinely better, more capable of civility.

PENNY SIMPSON, *Burnaby, British Columbia*

Peter gave me a sense of a definition of Canada. Through a thousand interviews, often just snapshots of the apparently mundane, these were the details of a country. This is us . . . details. Us making soup, surviving a flood, writing a Giller Prize–winning book, clearing the streets of snow. Us as intelligent, curious, creative.

What Trudeau advanced as an ideology of Canada, Gzowski displayed with the details. His unabashed nationalism and respect for everyone he talked with gave us a kaleidoscope of images with which to see and define our land and ourselves in a vernacular more dignified, intelligent, hip, fun and rich than I ever understood before. Trudeau made the loom, Gzowski the fabric. When the cloth was done, it was more than multicultural, more than just a good show.

BARRY BUCKNELL, *Grande Prairie, Alberta*

People have been saying that the Canada of Peter Gzowski is gone. That's simply not true. Peter's Canada is very much alive. It is alive in the towns, the cities, the suburbs, the bush, the farms, from coast to coast to coast. Those Canadian stories and values are still there, waiting to be heard. They may be dimmer, shouted down by louder voices in a public square that is becoming less public. But they are there nonetheless. That is to my mind Peter's greatest legacy: He showed us the wonder that is Canada. It is our task to not only protect that, but to tell its stories to a new generation, so they too will feel the love and wonder he experienced for this country.

THE REVEREND CHRISTOPHER WHITE, *Oshawa, Ontario*

Peter Gzowski was Canada. He embodied everything that was great about this country. He knew its poets, its athletes, its heartbreak and its glory. This is a vast country, and it is quite astounding that this simple man could understand and reflect the aspirations of farmers driving their tractors in the Prairies, Inuit in their huts in the far north and east coast fishermen on the high seas. I once argued, before I knew Gzowski, at an application to abandon certain rail lines, that if the ribbon of steel which once bound Canada together was severed, the only thing left to unite the country would be Peter Gzowski. I believed what I said and everyone in the room knew exactly what I was talking about.

FRANK MCKENNA, *Moncton, New Brunswick*

Peter, you inspired me to write, you inspired me to think outside of the borders, you taught me Canadian history, and you made me proud to be Canadian. Your books have kept me company on long flights around the world, and I left those books behind to be read by people in Colombia, Chile, Spain and Scotland. I have laughed with you, cried with you, agreed with you and disagreed, but always you made me think.

BRIAN HAM, *via e-mail*

Peter Gzowski gave me a glimpse of the liberal arts degree I was never going to have. He talked with people I wished I could have met and about things I wished I could know more about. The show was always about learning for me, not so much about facts or tangible things, but about people, from authors to hockey players, fishermen to professors. In a coffee room full of guys looking at the page three Sunshine girl, he was a light out of the darkness.

MERLE ELGERT, *Edmonton*

I am not a well-educated man, having managed to slumber my way through Grade 12. Peter and *Morningside* helped to fill that gap. I do not feel out of place in a discussion about Canadian authors, the performing arts and our rich Canadian landscape. I know there are thousands of his students across our great land who share the same thoughts and feelings.

JIM DUGGAN, *French River, Prince Edward Island*

In my early twenties when all my friends were at universities across the country and I was home here in Ottawa spending my days studying the guitar and listening to Peter, I used to joke that I was attending "Morningside U," majoring in "learning about Canada." The CBC is a great university, and Peter was the best classmate anyone could have wished for.

ALEX HOUGHTON, *Ottawa*

Peter taught me three things. One: Canada, with its vast beauty and regional differences, is a truly remarkable place to call home. Two: It is perfectly fine to be ordinary and intellectual at the same time. Three: Ordinary can be quite extraordinary.

May I be as respectful of people as I continue my Canadian journey.

SID ANDREWS, *Gananoque, Ontario*

When I last spoke to Peter Gzowski, I had called to say
how much I had enjoyed a recent column he had written for
the *Globe and Mail*. We went on to talk about the war in
Afghanistan, and my dislike of it, and then about journalism
and its present condition. His voice was hoarse and his breath
laboured. He was plainly unwell. Still, he was cheerful, went
on to talk of a column he planned to write about Stephen
Lewis, Eric Kierans and me, who had been with him on the
weekly political panel for more than a decade on *Morningside*.

And then, after a long hard fight, he was dead of emphysema. The country mourned its loss and celebrated his life.
In the genuine outpouring of sorrow, the sincerity of feeling,
like the man himself, was genuine and honest. People really
cared. The sense of loss was palpable. Peter was a unique presence, and there would not be anyone else like him, no one
even close.

I have been trying to explain to myself why so many
Canadians loved Peter Gzowski. What was the source of this
deep profound affection, this overflowing sentiment and sense
of loss? Odd that I have never heard anyone call him "Mr.
Gzowski." He was "Peter" to everyone, even to people who
had never met him, never knew him, but somehow had only
known him as Peter. I called him Peter, like everyone else. I
knew the gracious host of *Morningside*, the Canadian patriot,
the unabashed enthusiast, a man so many called a "great
Canadian" and meant all of it.

We did not talk easily, Peter Gzowski and I. For all the
charm, as well as we knew him, however much he became
familiar to us, there was an inner reserve, a mask that covered
the gregarious man. I used to watch him in crowds, position-
ing himself away from public scrutiny; he was very private, as
well as highly visible. He was, in fact, shy.

Peter was a teacher. He had the art of listening; he really did want to know what you thought. Radio, of course, is for listening. Dialogue is not monologue, and Peter Gzowski fashioned his career knowing the difference.

People trusted him, the listener in him enhanced his credibility, his audience trusted him, liked his quirky sense of humour – the joke was never on them. They believed he enjoyed small towns and ordinary people, and there was not a grain or dram of condescension in him. So almost everyone liked him and about as many people plain loved him.

Now we get to the important part and what made him so special. Peter Gzowski loved Canada, which is an awkward statement on a subject that makes a lot of us uneasy. Making love to a whole country, as beautiful as this one, is hard to do, especially for Canadians in the event someone else may be looking, or listening. Peter Gzowski, brave and resolute, was an irrepressible Canadian. Loving his country was no big deal. It was easy for Peter, who was born that way, the same as many of us, but in almost a lifetime showing it off, parading it about the country, he made a lot of converts.

We have learned from the death of Peter Gzowski something of ourselves. One is the depth of caring in the country. There is a vast majority out there that prefers gentleness to rancour, civility to belligerence. As for our future as a nation, our friend Peter, it would seem, has helped to encourage us to work to hang on for yet a while and hold on to what we have. Can anyone think of anybody who has done more than Peter Gzowski in that work of building national pride?

One may only guess how all this adulation would strike Peter. He would surely know he had become a Canadian icon in a nation of admirers who saw him as a national treasure. Still, on his death, we need to be reminded of the magnitude of our loss. It says something about this country that it could produce so towering a figure of such humility and grace, and also that Peter Gzowski would be recognized and cherished by so many of his fellow citizens.

I have been struck by the number of people who, in their tributes to Peter, almost unfailingly marked his contribution to national understanding and the building of national pride. These few sad days have helped to lend some confidence in the challenge we must confront in these times of corporate homogeneity and media convergence and the dark face of a rising capitalism, deeply lined by corruption and greed. What I mean to say is that a *country* of such spirit and knowing may honour the memory of our friend Peter by its determination to uphold the values, decency and loyalty to a country so distinguished by his life.

DALTON CAMP

Golfing on Ice

For months, I have thought about volunteering with our local Project Literacy group. I phoned them today.

— *JUDITH GUNDERSON, Kelowna, British Columbia*

We first met Peter when he came up to Pond Inlet for the Peter Gzowski Invitational Golf Tournament for Literacy in 1989. The idea for a northern PGI started with a conversation Peter had with Dorothy Komangapik. He fondly recalled his now famous conversation with Dorothy in a speech he wrote for the Pangnirtung PGI this past spring:

> "Say," she said, "aren't you the guy who runs those golf tournaments for literacy in the south?"
>
> "Yes," I said.
>
> "Well, how about up here," she said, "where we really need it?"
>
> "Excuse me," I said, "you have no golf courses."
>
> "Well, if you'll come," she said, "we'll build you one."
>
> So we came. And today you saw what Dorothy meant.

We've now had courses from Inuvik to Pond Inlet, from Fort Providence to Cambridge Bay and so many places in between. The golf has been both surprisingly good (don't forget there are course records all across the North that will never be broken because the courses have melted) and impossibly hilarious – if there were trophies for laughter we'd win them all.

Peter's direct involvement in the northern PGIs was one of the biggest reasons for their success. It is also the reason we all loved him so much. Peter helped us choose the guests, making sure the people who attended would be respectful of the northern culture and way of life. He made sure the guests were also people whom Nunavummiut would feel comfortable with. He helped us put the spotlight on literacy as an issue that affects all Nunavummiut.

When you add up the time Peter actually spent in Nunavut it wouldn't amount to more than a couple of months but whenever he arrived it was like a homecoming. We didn't think of him as a visitor because he really "got it." He understood our people and our politics as well as anyone here. As Shuvinai Mike, one of the Nunavut Literacy Council's board members, said, Peter's respect for Inuit and his love of Nunavut have made a difference in all of our lives.

Recently one of our staff members was organizing an event involving a celebrity. As she was going out the door, she said to her children that she was going to meet with a very important person. Her son Colin, eight years old at the time, said, "More important than Peter Gzowski?"

Peter came to Nunavut whenever he could, bringing the PGI and its famous entourage to Pond Inlet, Cambridge Bay, Iqaluit, Rankin Inlet and Kugluktuk. He was despondent that his health prevented him from going to Pangnirtung for the 2001 tournament. Premier Paul Okalik phoned Peter on the night before the golf game to say how much we would all miss him.

Peter asked actor Jonathan Torrens to read the speech on his behalf. Jonathan, a talented, well-known celebrity in his own right, was in awe of Peter and was very honoured and proud of the fact that Peter had asked him to read the speech. The Pangnirtung tournament was the first PGI in Nunavut Peter missed.

In 1999, when the Nunavut Literacy Council held its founding conference, Peter flew in to attend. At that time his emphysema was making it quite difficult for him to get around. For most people, the founding of our council was a fairly inconsequential event, but for Peter it was an important part of the creation of the new territory. For the board of directors, staff and members of the Nunavut Literacy Council, it meant a great deal.

Peter was not a typical celebrity. He was quite shy and when you first met him appeared to be somewhat of a curmudgeon. When Peter was in Nunavut, that famous Gzowski shyness was never apparent. Peter and our leaders were on a comfortable first-name basis. He said it was one of the greatest honours of his life to be asked to co-host the April 1, 1999, celebrations of the creation of the new Nunavut Territory. He often said that day was one of the most exciting days of his life: "I think of it still with pleasure and with pride."

Our good friend Bernadette Dean, an e-mail buddy of Peter's, would write to him when she was worried about her dad, would send Peter a jar of her home-made cranberry chutney and would drop in to visit him in Toronto with Aupilardjuk – one of Nunavut's famous elders – in tow, knowing that Peter would be delighted to see them. Bernadette says Peter was one of Nunavut's greatest ambassadors in the South. She's right.

In the speech Peter wrote for the Pangnirtung PGI he said, "Right now, I'm thinking of Mariano Aupilardjuk, and the *pissiq* he made at the Rankin Inlet PGI about caring for other people. You may have caught a glimpse of it when he performed it for the Aboriginal Achievement Awards telecast last month. It was and is a powerful statement. His spirit – and mine – are with you now."

Well, Peter, you were right – your spirit will always be with us.

THE NUNAVUT LITERACY COUNCIL:
SANDY KUSUGAK, DAN PAGE, DEBBIE MENCHIONS,
SUE BALL, JULIA OGINA, ELIZABETH LYALL, CANDACE
WIWCHARYK, MAGGIE PUTULIK, SHUVINAI MIKE,
KIM CROCKATT, CAYLA CHENIER, JANET ONALIK

I was at home with my son in 1986 when I found out that my family was moving to Frobisher Bay. There was a liaison person in Edmonton whom people moving North could call with questions about life up there. My first and most important question was "Can you get *Morningside* in Frobisher Bay?" Yes.

Late in 1988 I was on the Library Board and we were looking for an author to come to Iqaluit (formerly Frobisher Bay). We were able to provide a $200 honorarium.

I was listening to *Morningside* when I suddenly got inspired, picked up the phone, got the number for the CBC in Toronto from Directory Assistance and asked to speak to Peter G. When they asked if they could say who was calling, I told them the truth – he wouldn't have a clue who I was, I was just a woman in Iqaluit who, along with all of her friends and our community, would love to meet him and have him speak to us and visit. A few hours later I got a phone call. Peter already had commitments in April of 1989, but he moved heaven and earth and came up to spend four days in Iqaluit and Pangnirtung for the princely sum of $200! Peter loved the North and delighted in this huge part of Canada and all of the peoples who live here.

He was a delightful guest and I am privileged that, for a few days, I got to spend time with this wonderful Canadian.

CATHERINE PELLERIN, *Yellowknife*

We sat on the bench in front of the Mackenzie Hotel in Inuvik doing a promo for the show I worked on. We talked about anything and everything. While the cameraman was shooting close-ups, wide shots, re-asks and everything else the producer conjured up, Peter patiently nodded and smiled at the appropriate times. We shared experiences and laughed at comical moments we experienced on TV. I met a Peter Gzowski I never saw on TV or heard on radio or listened to making a speech.

Peter and I marvelled at how Ernie Coombs handled the crowd in Fort Smith. We had just landed for another Peter Gzowski Invitational Golf Tournament. As the plane taxied to stop in front of the terminal building, we noticed hundreds of people in the building. There were mothers, fathers, grandmothers, grandfathers, sons, daughters, babies and even the family dogs and cats. They didn't notice me or Peter. We simply walked past them and waited for our luggage. They all came to see Mr. Dressup. They wanted autographs, photos, hugs or just to see the man who was Mr. TV to them. Later Peter would talk about the patience, the way Ernie handled the young people, the way Ernie took time for those who were no longer young but wanted some time with Mr. Dressup.

I was with Peter in Kugluktuk, formerly called Coppermine, when he did not look too good. He was coughing, hacking, and didn't take part in the golfing event. It was still winter in May. The ice and snow made golfing difficult. This was by far the toughest course I've ever played on but the long days with blue skies and sunshine made it all worthwhile. The people fussed over Peter; he told them not to worry. Despite how he looked or sounded, he made time for the local people. He spoke at the banquet, took part in the drum dance and encouraged everyone to learn the basics of reading, writing and listening.

I watched Peter in Yellowknife at another invitational golf tournament. He looked healthier. He even went out for a few rounds. I remember that year as the year my team had the best score. But what I remember most was Peter's reaction later. I watched him at a banquet as a man shared his story about how he learned to read and write. The man appeared to be in his thirties. He read to the assembled the story he had written about what life was like not being able to read or write. It was an emotional time. The man smiled broadly as he showed off his new-found skill. But the smile was nothing compared to what Peter Gzowski had on his face. Peter looked like he just scored the overtime goal in the seventh game of the Stanley Cup final.

As a writer and one who read a lot, Peter knew that if people were going to make it in this day and age, they needed the basics in reading and writing. He wished everyone in Canada could have that. He gave his time, his talents and his efforts to make that a reality but what made Peter unique was his yearning for learning, especially about the North. He always had a notebook, scraps of paper or a napkin to write on. He was always having discussions with someone, anyone. He would jot down something, then back to the conversation, then more scribbling. His interest in the North was always obvious. He was a student of life, he was giver more than taker and he was a man of action. In the few time I've seen him he made others richer. He often reminded me of my elders' teachings. They would say I don't want you to be rich, happy or famous. I just want you to be a good man. I knew he was famous. I don't know if he was rich or happy but he made me think, made me laugh and made me think of how I treat others. That, elders would say, is a sign of a good man.

PAUL ANDREW, *Yellowknife*

Mr. Gzowski invited me to be Poet Laureate at the Briars. I agreed to participate, with some trepidation. I was shepherded around the links on a golf cart by a very nice young woman with the idea that I would meet the guests and eventually write a poem based on my experience on the fairways and the greens. That afternoon I sat in Peter's cottage, writing my golf poem, a fond memory of a very generous and gentle and surprisingly shy man.

there you stood
guarding the green with that gentle voice
an almost handsome shambles
leaning on your putter
like something dressed to scare the human crows
a brown-trousered man
cinched by twine in time
here among the Brummel tweeds
and famous-fashioned sweaters

Peter of Green Gables.

PG and Gill at
Swallow Point,
Nova Scotia.

A peaceful moment, fly-fishing on the Miramichi, 1992.

A dramatic moment in the Caribbean described in *A Peter Gzowski Reader: The Vagrant*, dismasted, Antigua, winter 1984.

PG and Peter Howard, proud croquet winners at Swallow Point.

PG and Gill in a relaxed moment.

The sign outside the Red Barn Theatre, Jackson's Point, Ontario.

PG on the tee
at the PGI.

With
Sarah Polley
at the Red Barn,
1992.

With the cast of "Street Legal" at the Red Barn, 1992: Eric Peterson, Cynthia Dale, Anthony Sherwood, C. David Johnson, Julie Kahner.
Photo courtesy Terry Hancey

At the first PGI in Ottawa: left to right, Gerry White, Brad Munro, PG, Barry Turner, Paul Jones, John O'Leary, Richard Nolan, Joyce White.

The PGI proved to be very popular when it moved to the North. PG in his Pangnirtung hat in Yellowknife in 1990.

With Nellie Cournoyea in Yellowknife, 1990.

First time golf was played on the ice in Yellowknife, 1990.

Northern and Southern visitors to the golf course at Pond Inlet, 1991.

Cambridge Bay, 1994.

on the briar links
you threw down the dare
the dimpled ball
would ride the follows
up and down the physics
of an earth swell smoothing
for the hole
or close the hole
just shy a single roll
or wide, the tacking failure
going still
as a duck egg shouldered
by an orphan being born by wobbles from within
and so
we laugh at miracles
how they sometimes miss the mark
and bless the shadow
that we cast
where the loss-light
is a greater light
and we share in that
by being the stone-cooling simulacrum of the shade responding
where we've gone and where we go.

JOHN B. LEE, *Brantford, Ontario*

Lynn's memories: My adventures with Peter started with a phone call. Somehow I never quite expected to get a call that began with "Hello – this is Peter Gzowski." On the radio every morning, yes, but not on the end of my telephone at work! It was late November 1989, and during that first forty minutes on the phone we dreamed and planned what would become the Northern PGIs. Just a little different from those southern ones where they golfed on greens!

The first Northern PGI began a few months later in April 1990 when I met Peter in person at the Yellowknife airport. Peter – a rumpled, poppa-bear figure as familiar as family – emerging from the aircraft, leading a group of fourteen friends. It was the first time I realized how important it was to Peter that he be able to share and show off "his North." That night Peter took his friends for a walk under the magic of the aurora borealis – out on the golf course we had made for him of ice and snow.

The next year, 1991, I flew with Peter into Pond Inlet, high above the Arctic Circle. Once again he was leading a gathering of friends to promote the cause of literacy, which was so dear to his heart. The pilot, playing to his captive audience, circled low over the little town and out over the beautiful golf course we had built on the frozen Arctic Ocean – a golf course with a perfect iceberg "hazard" set in its midst. As we taxied on the snowy runway towards the small terminal building, it was obvious there was not a soul left in town – everyone was at the airport to meet Peter Gzowski. I would have worried about the local fire marshal (the terminal building was clearly filled beyond capacity) if he, too, were not focused on getting an autograph.

Over the next ten years this scene repeated itself annually, each year in a different community. The only Northern PGI that involved road travel was 1992 in Fort Providence. We had flown Peter and friends by jet to Yellowknife and then on a small Twin Otter aircraft to the PGI. When the time came to leave, we were in white-out blizzard conditions and the Twin Otter couldn't get to us. I hastily arranged for a school bus to attempt to get Peter to Yellowknife and the southbound jet.

The bus driver took his mission very seriously – Peter Gzowski had to make that jet – and drove like a wild man for two hundred kilometres in a blizzard on a narrow dirt road. This may have been one of the few times in his life Peter was truly unnerved. His stories on *Morningside* the following Monday about the "bus ride from hell" were particularly vivid.

We had many adventures together over the years, and I have wonderful memories, but there is one image that endures. I always see our Northern Peter hunched over in a chair, arms resting on his legs, hands clasped together, listening with rapt intensity to Inuit or Dene elders. An extraordinary storyteller himself, he found a deep pleasure in listening to the elders telling the stories that passed, from one generation to the next, the history, knowledge and wisdom of the people of the North. These were especially wonderful times, but none had quite the impact on Peter as when he met Leah Nutaruk – the eldest of the elders of Baffin Island. At that time she was 103, and her smile and the moment were magic. She told stories of Scottish whalers, her nomadic childhood on the land, the beauty of the mountains at Pangnirtung, what it was like to birth, love, raise and bury her five children. The poet Sheree Fitch was with Peter on that PGI, and she captured that moment in a poem that moved us deeply. Some years later, when Leah died, Peter marked her passing on *Morningside* and in her honour had Sheree read "Aurora Borealis" – her poem about Leah – on the program.

∞

Barb's memories: My earliest special memory of Peter happened years before I met him. I was a new mother, at home with my baby and my own mum, who had come to stay with us for a couple of weeks. My mum is a terrific knitter and was sitting in the living room with me as I nursed my baby and listened to *Morningside*. Peter was learning to knit on the air. Mum picked up a fresh pair of needles and a new ball of wool and followed the instructions of the knitting teacher. It was a new method for her of casting on stitches, and ever since she has called it the "Gzowski method." He said he never learned to knit a stitch that day, but I have always wondered how many other people across Canada did.

That was Peter's way. He never did completely realize the huge impact he, his radio show and his writing had on this country. Like those of many women, my memories of *Morningside* are all tangled up with my memories of motherhood: babies, cooking, Camp, Kierans and Lewis, toddlers, Stuart McLean and laundry.

I did finally meet my hero. I had the pleasure of organizing and attending several PGI golf tournaments. Those were magical events, communities putting on their best spit and polish, lots of fun, little sleep and meeting wonderful authors, actors and musicians from around the country.

A man he brought along to many of the Arctic golf tournaments, Mr. Dressup, eclipsed even Peter in stardom. Peter took huge pleasure in watching the superstar status of Ernie Coombs. I'm sure he was thinking, "How Canadian." Very few people know that Peter once made Mr. Dressup cry. He was presenting Ernie with the "Gzowski Award" at the 2000 PGI and in his speech said so many nice things about him that Ernie welled up. This had a sort of domino effect, and very soon everyone in the entire room, including Wayne Rostad, was weeping.

One of my fondest memories is of the time I took Peter G. grocery shopping. He was in Yellowknife for several weeks researching a book he was planning on the North and was staying at an apartment-hotel. I ran into him at a Literacy

Week breakfast and he mentioned that he needed to buy groceries. Well, I just happened to be on my way to the Co-op store after breakfast so I took him along. It was the most unusual grocery-shopping trip I've ever had – we couldn't go fifteen feet without someone stopping him, shaking his hand and telling him how much they enjoyed his work. Finally, we made it to the checkout. At our Co-op, membership is mandatory but a person can do a one-time trial shop. I went to a cashier and said, "This is my friend Peter Gzowski. He's here for a trial shop." Well, it turned out she was the only one in the store who didn't know him. She inquired if he would like a membership package to learn all about the benefits of joining the Yellowknife Co-op. Others might have said they were just here temporarily, or even "Don't you know who I am?" But not Peter. Without a moment's hesitation he said yes, he would take a package. When I dropped him off at his apartment, he took his groceries and his membership package in – and I bet he read it.

Once I organized a Gzowski book signing at our local bookstore. A long line of people waited patiently to get their books signed, but more than that, to talk with Peter. He often said that everyone in the North has a story to tell, and that day he heard lots of them. Many people wanted to tell him of connections they had with him or how he had impacted their lives.

∽

What he meant to us: And that was what Peter was about – he told Canadians our stories on *Morningside* and in print while somehow, at the same time, he changed us a little bit, made us all a little better. Peter Gzowski was as important to us as our stories were to him.

It is impossible to imagine anyone other than Peter who would know about Leah Nutaruk or who could tell so many stories of the North and its people. Who else could understand the importance to us as a national community that these stories be told? Who else could tell our stories with such grace and affection? He wrote with eloquence and passion on the importance of the "idea" of the North to all of Canada. And we accepted him as one of us because he drew us into the larger Canadian community, and in that larger community he validated our experiences, and because he so obviously felt at home in our part of Canada.

He enriched our lives and provided us with adventures and experiences we never would have had without him. He became our friend, and we loved him – as simple as that.

LYNN FOGWILL AND BARB PAQUIN, *Yellowknife*

Peter came to Kugluktuk for the Peter Gzowski golf tournament when I was teaching high school. My students did not come to school that day, as they were too excited about Mr. Dressup and some hockey players who had accompanied Peter. They were all out watching the golf tournament. Peter's back was too sore to golf, and I noticed him sitting in our small library checking out our books. I went and sat with him and was so blessed to have the chance to chat with him, just the two of us, for about two hours. I know many, many Canadians will miss him but I think those of us who live in small places in the corners of Canada will miss him the most.

MINDY WILLETT, *Yellowknife*

One of my most special memories of Peter dates to 1994, the first year the Nova Scotia PGI was held in Cape Breton, and

George Unsworth and I were co-chairing the event. It's almost hard to remember a time when East Coast music wasn't hot, but only a few artists were well-known a decade ago. We decided on a hillside outdoor concert at Dundee the afternoon before, with the very deliberate thought that we wanted to introduce more of our fantastic musicians to Peter, Rita MacNeil and the Rankins being among the few who had made it to national attention by then.

The day was overcast turning to sunny, but the three-plus hours of music were magic . . . there were the Barra MacNeils, Natalie McMaster, Cyril MacPhee and Brakin' Tradition, John Gracie, the Sons of Membertou, Jo-Anne Rolls, Joel Chiasson and a yet-unfamous young fellow by the name of Ashley MacIsaac, among others. Murray McLauchlan was along for the afternoon ride, too, since – can you believe it? – we felt we needed a headliner because the other names were still so little known off the island.

Peter lapped it up. The following day of the golf tournament dawned bright and pristine over the lakes, and we all clambered over the mountain-goat verticals of the Dundee course. That night, we tackled mountains of lobster and steak under a tent overlooking a once-a-decade sunset light show over Marble Mountain and the Bras d'Or. Neil Black and I drank enough wine to start the step-dancing, and the party went on for hours.

In the end, we raised more money for literacy than had any other single PGI tournament to date. Very satisfying – but the other satisfying bit was that, over the next year, Peter played on air the music of every group and solo performer from the Sunday afternoon hillside ceilidh, and interviewed many of them. His nascent love affair with East Coast music burst into full bloom, and the Canadian Celtic revival has never looked back.

Fortunately, as all Cape Bretoners know, heaven is full of fiddlers, so Peter will feel right at home.

JACQUELYN THAYER SCOTT, *Ben Eoin, Cape Breton, Nova Scotia*

In 1999, I met Peter for the first time. We were living in Kugluktuk, Nunavut, and I was serving as chairperson of the PGI committee. Kugluktuk had the honour of hosting the first PGI tournament for literacy in Nunavut, which had become an official territory April 1, 1999. Peter's presence was in doubt due to poor health. To our great pleasure, we were informed a couple of weeks prior to the tournament that Peter would be coming to Kugluktuk. However, we were also advised that he could be a "bit of a curmudgeon" and that we should be prepared to cater to him.

We met the plane with not a little trepidation, but any fears we might have had quickly dissolved. Despite coping with a painful back condition, he was a very gracious guest and gave freely and enthusiastically of his time to young and old. I was most impressed by his kindness, his warmth and his humble presence. The three days in Kugluktuk seemed to rejuvenate him, and he appeared to get as much from the community as the community received from his presence.

TOM STEWART, *Kugluktuk, Nunavut*

I saw him on several occasions in the nineties at the PGI tournaments and when I received a Learner Award. He was a quiet man, sitting with his cigarette and Scotch, enjoying everything around him.

Gzowski gave me the opportunity to continue. He showed me that perseverance works and that there was hope in learning. Peter Gzowski gave learners hope through literacy and in turn literacy allowed him to be humble.

MURD NICHOLSON, *Yukon*

Peter Gzowski and I met a long time ago in his CBC studio and then in Yellowknife during his March 2000 golf tournament for literacy. Golfing lasted three hours, but the three-day literacy festival inspired hundreds of people from kindergarten to high school, from adult education centres to retirement homes. On the last day I was invited to say something at the banquet. Here is what I said:

Tommy has been living on the fringe of Yellowknife and we've been friends for thirty years. Yesterday we happened to meet at the Gold Range coffee shop.

"René, when did you come from Lutsel K'e?"

"Two days ago. I came to watch the Yellowknife golf tourn –"

"Nobody says Yellowknife gulf, it is Yellowknife bay."

"I don't mean gulf, it's golf, G-O-L-F."

"What's that?"

"It's a game. Each player has one ball."

"They have only one ball!"

"Yes, a rubber ball this big, and each golfer has a club."

"Canadian Club?"

"No! A club is a stick to hit the ball with."

"Why do they want to hit a ball?"

"They start hitting the ball from one place, and far away there is a cup."

"A cup to drink what?"

"They say a 'cup,' but it's only a hole in the ground.
Golfers hit their ball until it drops into the cup. A lucky player
can get a hole in one."

"What a sweet dream! René, how come you know so
much? Did you play golf before?"

"Tommy, I never played golf, but I am lucky: I learned to
read. Yesterday at the library, I picked up a book about golf; I
know only what I read but tomorrow I'll watch the golf tournament on the ice of Frame Lake. They cleared the snow here
and there."

"It could be fun after all."

"If you come with me tomorrow, we'll learn about golf
together."

So this afternoon, Tommy and I wandered from holes 1
to 9.

"Tommy, those golfers are going for the tee."

"Is that what they drink?"

"A tee, T-E-E, is the starting point, and each player has
a driver."

"To drive them where?"

"Nowhere! They're going to walk. Their club is called
a driver."

"Will they play with those yellow tennis balls?"

"Probably easier to find in the snow."

The ball flew . . . shshsh . . . Tommy was impressed.

"Wow! Fran got the ball so close to the hole."

"A good golfer! And now she can shoot an eagle."

"Have you ever seen an eagle here in March?"

"In golf language it means that she goes faster than the
average player."

"I heard Joe complain that the greens are too hard. What's
that?"

"A green is the space around a hole, but here the green is clear ice."

"Gee, those people don't speak English as we do."

Tommy met Mr. Dressup, Ernie Coombs.

"Do you golf for fun?"

"Yes, I enjoy it, and besides, it's the only way I could come to Yellowknife this year."

"René, who is that guy way over there at number 7? He's jumping all over the place and shouting, 'I made it, I made it. I can never be humble again!'"

"I don't know, ask around."

Suzette answered Tommy: "I cannot see that far, but this thunder sounds like Wayne Rostad."

And Diane said, "I'm kind of deaf, but this windmill looks like Wayne."

And then the golf tournament was over.

"Well, René, you remember when you lived in Yellowknife, I used to bum a few dollars from you for a six-pack or a bottle of wine?"

"Yes, I remember."

"Well, I don't need any money for booze, but if you can spare a twenty I'm gonna buy myself an English dictionary."

RENÉ FUMOLEAU, *Lutsel'ke, Great Slave Lake, Northwest Territories*

When my children, two of whom make up the Peters Drury Trio, were extended an invitation to play for the PGI gala, I understood the gift that was being offered to them. Peter introduced them that night in the forty-plus-degree temperatures: "You'll be surprised at several things about the next group. Their ages – fifteen and seventeen – and where they are from – the Yukon." The performance was not without a glitch: Jesse's microphone didn't work. These three young musicians didn't bat an eye. After the mike was replaced, Jesse, all of seventeen years old, calmly said to the audience, "It's like the song says, 'Love Is Better the Second Time Around,' so here we go!" The audience loved it.

The next day, as we went to say our goodbyes, Peter looked at Jesse and said, "You know we did that on purpose, just to test you!" And then he smiled.

That fall, when the kids released their first CD, Peter sent words of congratulations to be read at the concert in Whitehorse. "Way to go, you guys. I know that some day, because of your wonderful appearance at the Red Barn, I'll be able (and proud) to say I knew you when."

DEBBIE PETERS, *Whitehorse, Yukon*

When I heard the news about Peter Gzowski's death, the memories of various experiences with him came flooding back. Writing from 2,500 kilometres away, I see him in many places and many ways.

There was the letter, a few lines scrawled on CBC notepaper. This was about fifteen years ago, after I'd written a *Globe and Mail* column on golf in November. I played the Glen Abbey Golf Club on my own while carrying my clubs. This is golf at its best – walking and playing a fine course quickly, in bracing air.

A couple of days later a letter arrived from Gzowski. An avid listener to *Morningside* on CBC Radio, I'd been taken with Gzowski's love of reading and feeling for sport. He wasn't afraid to think of sports writing as real writing. To him, good sports writing belonged as much on the books and cultural pages as the sports pages.

"I've been thinking about writing a book on golf," Gzowski wrote. "But I read your column this morning. You write the book."

When he started his tournaments to raise money for literacy in Canada in 1986, he invited me to play. Maestro ballstriker George Knudson also played. Knudson, like Gzowski on Thursday, succumbed to the ravages of lifelong smoking in 1989.

Gzowski appreciated the way Knudson hit the ball – pure, without a hitch, flowing through to his target in balance. He liked Knudson's simple feelings for golf as play and recreation. (Oddly enough, both Gzowski and Knudson died on January 24, and that morning two days ago, Knudson's wife, Shirley, welcomed the birth of her second granddaughter, Georgia.)

Knudson, to Gzowski, embodied the principle of golf. He tried to help Gzowski swing better. Gzowski knew the game, having played it as a kid with family at the Briars Golf and Country Club in Jackson's Point, Ontario, on Lake Simcoe, where he and his companion, the gracious Gill Howard, now had a cottage.

Gzowski had returned to golf at what was truly his home course, to raise money for literacy – his well-known Peter Gzowski Invitationals started at the Briars. He said at the first PGI that he had committed to raising a million dollars for literacy through golf.

"I wrote the promise down on a Scotch-stained napkin," Gzowski would always say. John O'Leary, the president of Frontier College and the man who first asked Gzowski to help out with literacy issues in Canada, is glad he did, as are communities across Canada.

The PGIs soon played across the country and have raised seven million dollars; they constitute a truly Canadian tour. Gzowski travelled to the tournaments and ensured there were Canadian connections at each one – actors, comedians, writers, musicians.

The tournaments were boisterous fun. I played with Jack McClelland, the founder of McClelland & Stewart, who played with clubs vintage 1940 or so, and rattled the ball around the Briars with gusto. There were memorable rounds with the first-class sports writers – and Canadian treasures – Scott Young and Trent Frayne. Friendships that endure were formed.

The PGIs were creative acts, and Gzowski always credited members of his team, especially his assistant, Shelley Ambrose. Consider one event in Yellowknife on a frozen lake in April, in the early 1990s. It represented an impressive feat of organization.

Ken Dryden was there, as was the gifted actress Cynthia Dale. We walked out onto the frozen lake to watch the northern lights the night before the tournament, teed it up with orange golf balls on the ice the next day where holes three feet square had been cut, warmed ourselves with tea and stronger liquids on each tee, ate toasty bannock, the local bread, and had a blast. Gzowski and others read to kids at a local school one afternoon. By then, Gzowski had established the Knudson award at the PGI. A silver tee was given in Knudson's name to the person whom Gzowski deemed had the most fun during his or her round. To heck with the score. The Knudson was the most important award at each PGI. Still is.

Meanwhile, I had taken up on Gzowski's suggestion in his letter two decades ago that I write books. He provided a foreword to my collection *Touring Prose*, and, recalling one of our rounds at the Briars, wrote, "We had our usual pleasant time." We sure did.

On *Morningside*, a salon for writers, Gzowski had me on a couple of times to talk golf writing. He generously made me the first writer-in-residence for the Briars PGI. Another year he made Canadian golf writer John Gordon the writer-in-residence. Gzowski championed our work.

As writer-in-residence, my only responsibility was to write an essay about golf and writing and the ways in which they link with each other, which I did and called it "In Peaceful Communion." It sounds corny just as a title, but together on an evening playing golf at the Briars, Gzowski and I knew that the game did offer a peaceful communion – with friends, with nature, with our quiet selves, at play.

Now Gzowski is gone, at sixty-seven. He would probably have cracked that it's a good number, at least in golf. Knudson is gone. But their influence remains, firm, encouraging. Gzowski connected with Canadians, and he helped us connect, on and off the course.

LORNE RUBENSTEIN, *Toronto*

Most of all, we were so impressed with the manner in which Peter was able to talk to people. You could tell by the sparkle in his eyes that he truly loved the stories of the North. With such an impressive background of interviews, he had the ability to make you feel as if you were in his living room enjoying a nice Sunday chat (even if you were talking about eating muskrats for dinner!).

In an interview with us in Fort Providence, we were amazed how comfortable he made us both feel and by the end of the interview, we were all laughing at stories told. Peter was an incredible ambassador to the North and in his own way was able to let people from across the country realize that although the North is an interesting part of the world, it is the people of the North and their stories which make this part of the country such a beautiful place.

JOE AND JANE DRAGON, *Yellowknife*

In the 1970s I flew overnight to Toronto for my very first TV interview on Peter Gzowski's show. I was very young, sleep-deprived and talked too slowly for TV but I enjoyed Peter and his other guest Otto Preminger who being bald admired me for my hair!

When Peter came for his first NWT Golf Tournament for Literacy, I had a small conflict as a Dene leader. That day I had a choice . . . go golfing with Peter Gzowski or attend the initialling of the Dene/Metis comprehensive land claim agreement! Peter often laughed about my remark: When my children ask me years from now, "Where were you, Dad, when the agreement was initialled?" will I tell them I was out golfing?

STEPHEN KAKFWI, *Yellowknife*

Since the first PGI in 1986, Peter Gzowski raised almost seven million dollars for literacy programs, raised public awareness about the cause and recruited thousands of new literacy volunteers. There is now a PGI in each province and territory and one designated for aboriginal languages and literacy.

Recently some friends were talking about Peter and the *Morningside* years and someone asked, "How did Peter get involved with literacy anyway?"

"I can answer that," I said.

I was in the Ben Wicks bar on Parliament Street on a grey, windy afternoon in November 1985. I was in despair.

As president of Frontier College, Canada's original literacy organization, I was trying to raise public awareness about literacy. I was getting nowhere. Federal and provincial governments were indifferent to the issue, the private sector was totally ignorant about it, and the general public was highly sceptical. A prominent bookseller of the time had thrown me out of his office: "I'm selling books, for crying out loud, why the hell should I care about literacy?" I was about ready to give up when Janet Turnbull Irving, a friend and then publisher of Seal Books, said that she'd heard something on *Morningside* about reading and writing.

Morningside! Book reviews, authors, intelligent, literate conversation. Perfect. And then Peter published the first *Morningside Papers*. Here were these wonderful letters and essays from Peter's listeners in big cities and small towns and from every part of Canada.

The Morningside Army. An army of potential volunteers and advocates for literacy! And who better than Peter Gzowski, man of letters and vendor of words, to lead the crusade?

I wrote out a five-page proposal and sent it off to Peter. "The Morningside Army: a proposal to mobilize the Morningside Army of readers and writers to get Canada reading again!"

What a brilliant idea, I thought. Peter can't say no.

Peter said no.

He wrote back and explained how his job and his responsibility to literacy and to other important causes were to "do the best radio we can" about them. Then he added: "I hesitate to mention a totally different subject to you. But one of the things at the back of my mind . . . is a plan to run a golf tournament (the Peter Gzowski Invitational?) for a worthy cause, and literacy has crossed my mind . . . do you think Frontier College would think about being involved?"

I called Peter right away. "You bet we would be interested in a golf tournament!" Peter was delighted and we agreed to meet to start planning but I remember thinking, right after hanging up the phone, "How the hell do you run a golf tournament?"

Well, we didn't know how. Neither did Peter. But we did it anyway. That is, Peter did it. Everyone he called and asked to help out came through for us. The golf pro at the Briars organized the tournament, Premier David Peterson (a former Frontier College instructor) came to kick things off with a shotgun start, Peter's friends and associates, from Ken Dryden (who hates golf) to Lorne Rubenstein (a professional golfer and author), all agreed to attend. Peter's prominence enabled us to line up some great prizes. Lovecraft, in Yorkville, was a prize sponsor – "We love Peter Gzowski. His show is on in the store all the time" – and Peter made the rules, including the inclusion of the first-ever poet laureate at a golf tournament. That year, it was Dennis Lee, author, poet laureate of Toronto and another former Frontier literacy teacher.

I have rarely worked so hard or laughed so much as at that first PGI. And, at the end of the day, at Peter's family cottage, we all savoured the moment. We had raised badly needed funds for Frontier College, we had informed an influential group of people about the cause and we had had a wonderful, memorable day. Peter looked at me and said, "We should do this again."

"I'm holding you to that," I said. Then I grabbed a whisky-stained napkin from the table and scribbled: "I, Peter Gzowski, will raise $1 million for literacy in Canada." Peter signed, with Janet Turnbull as the witness.

That was sixteen years, 150 tournaments, three prime ministers, a dozen premiers and 150 poet laureates ago. The great generosity and the commitment to literacy generated at that first PGI has burst out across Canada. Peter is gone now, but his PGIs are continuing.

And the real measurement of the PGIs' success is the thousands of people, in every part of our country, who are now reading, writing and delighting in the words and the language that Peter Gzowski loved so dearly and employed so well.

JOHN O'LEARY, *Toronto*

"Lines Read at the Peter Gzowski Golf Tournament for Literacy, July 10, 2002"

A tiny object, circular,
A sudden burst of energy,
Toward a tiny flag afar –
To rise, to soar for all to see.
To tumble like a falling star,
To disappear beneath the ground,
Not goodbye but au revoir:
A game of golf is called a round.
There is a figure, call it par
To tell us who the winners are.

A smoke is smoked, a throat is cleared,
A candid heart, a spacious mind,
Spectacles, a shaggy beard,
While in a studio confined,
Across an entire land appeared.

A mind, a voice, a thought, a word,
Soared across the atmosphere
Into an ear it fell, was heard.
He golfed through half the continent
To find out where his broadcast went.

His game he played, his life he led,
Yet who remembers what occurred?
Of what was done and what was said,
What left except the written word?
A voice is stilled, a body shed,
A mind remembered as a thought,
He is never wholly dead,
As long as reading can be taught.
A round is played, the score is read,
A shaggy cloud flies overhead.

JOHN MacLACHLAN GRAY, *Vancouver*

Mr. Chancellor

One thing that stands out about the day I received my degree is the handshake and sincere congratulations I received from Mr. Gzowski. In that sea of other eager, equally deserving students, he made me feel as if I really mattered.

— *JENNIFER DAVIDSON, Waterloo, Ontario*

Great commencement address fondly remembered . . . my oh my, Mr. Gzowski rocks!

— *SASHA FURLANI, Toronto*

I am a fourth-year honours student at Trent.

For years I worked alone in my home and listened to CBC Radio daily. *Morningside* was my favourite show. Peter Gzowski's beautiful voice, along with the theme song, will forever be etched in my memory.

Last year I had the opportunity to spend two hours in an intimate seminar setting with Peter Gzowski and about twenty other students here at Trent. The class, Canada: The North, was instructed by Professor Manore. We were briefed in advance about the fact that we would be given the rare privilege of picking Peter Gzowski's brain, about his experiences in Canada's northern regions, and also that it would be his first public appearance since becoming extremely ill with emphysema.

The room became very quiet. Reverence and anticipation seemed to fill the air when he entered. He walked very slowly all the way across the room with his oxygen tanks trailing behind him and sat down right beside me. Before he could begin to speak, there were a few very long moments while he caught his breath. I can remember thinking how difficult this must be for him and wondering if I would be brave enough to take on a class of university students under the same conditions.

When he did speak, his breathing was still laboured but his voice was soothing. He thanked us for our patience and then explained that this was his first public appearance with, as he described them, "the hoses in his nose," and added that he was feeling very self-conscious. He then went on to tell us that he had destroyed his lungs by smoking cigarettes and joked about the fact that he would make a good advertisement, at this point, for an anti-smoking campaign.

I felt humbled by his candour. I was struck by his ability to present himself in a weakened state with such gentle accept-ance. I think this is a rare quality in a human being.

He said he would like this meeting to be very relaxed and open, and that he would like to start with questions from us, and that we could go ahead and ask him anything. Well, we all just sat there staring. Nobody said a word for quite a long time, until he finally broke the ice by saying, "Well, I guess this isn't going to work so maybe I'll just start talking and we will see what happens."

What followed was a lively and thoroughly informative overview of Canada's North, beginning in the late twentieth century and ending with a detailed discussion of the inception of Nunavut. For me, the most memorable moment in this seminar was when Peter Gzowski was asked about northern women and politics. He described the gender parity issue in Nunavut and the fact that a plebiscite on the issue had taken place, and that the idea had been turned down. I hadn't heard about the issue of gender parity until that moment and had no idea of the complexities, or even of the general history, of Inuit women's dilemmas in terms of political representation, but I

was intrigued, so I asked, "Why do you think they voted no?"
He paused for a moment and then looked me right in the eye
and said, "Well, I really don't know."

What a great moment of inspiration that was for me. I
thought, if Peter Gzowski doesn't know, then this will make a
great topic for my paper. I wrote that paper. I learned a lot
about northern politics, Inuit culture, gender parity and on top
of all that I won the Symons award for the best Canadian
Studies essay.

I would like to take this opportunity to thank Peter
Gzowski for inspiring me to reach well beyond my perceived
capacity in the investigation of understanding what it means to
be a Canadian, for demonstrating how to be courageous and
humble at the same time, and for being honest.

Thanks, Peter.

LYNDA MANNIK, *Peterborough, Ontario*

Peter Gzowski and I wore many hats together. We had a professional relationship during the years I was president of
McClelland & Stewart, which published his books. He was a
model author, always willing to do whatever we asked to
promote his books. And he did more to promote the books of
other authors than anyone in the country. We shared the love
of and commitment to Canadian writing and writers.

We also had a personal relationship that manifested itself
on more than one golf course, including the one we set up
inside a motel in northern Canada, when the PGI on ice was
thawed out. The most difficult hole was the last. A short pitch
from our motel to the bar across the street, onto the pool table
and into the corner pocket. You can assume that we didn't
leave the bar once the final shot had been made.

But the relationship on which I would like to focus was our collegial one, as chancellors of two fine universities – Trent University and York University.

I was very pleased when Peter called to ask my advice when he was offered the position of chancellor at Trent. I told him that he should accept at once and that he would find it one of the most rewarding activities he had ever undertaken. I was gratified when my advice proved to be so prescient.

We shared a commitment to a view of education that has fallen out of favour recently. Peter and I both believed passionately in the value of a broad liberal arts education. Neither of us could quite buy into the idea that universities are career-training shops, as opposed to environments within which to explore all aspects of learning. Universities are for expanding our options, not for shutting them down and narrowing our focus. Peter and I even shared the view that there's a great deal of significant education to be found outside the classroom – even in the campus coffee shops and pubs. Perhaps that's why neither of us earned an undergraduate degree. And we agreed that one of the greatest benefits of a university education is the development of the love of learning. There are those these days who condemn this kind of thinking as being impractical, but I would suggest that the critics of this philosophy might want to consider Peter's life and career, which in many ways exemplified this philosophy of education.

He was a learner all of his life. His infectious curiosity was what made him such a great journalist and broadcaster. His range of interests was as vast as the country itself, and the relentless enthusiasm with which he approached the people and things that interested him made even those Canadians who only knew his voice want to know more about them, too.

Peter's education ended much too early, but during the time he had, he changed how we see this country. And he changed it by keeping his mind open and by following his curiosity wherever it took him. Come to think of it, that's not a bad model for the kind of education he believed in. And look what he achieved! Maybe it wasn't so impractical after all.

AVIE BENNETT, *Toronto*

I had the opportunity to meet Peter during his time as chancellor of Trent University. He visited campus often and was always keen to meet with students to discuss our passions and why we chose Trent. Even in poor health he had the courage to visit Trent to meet with community members during some of the most tense political debates on the future of our school. He always offered important interventions about the importance of what goes on at a liberal arts and sciences university like Trent and gave all of us important perspective even during the most heated debates.

The memory of Peter Gzowski that will last with me forever was from this past June when he conferred upon me a Bachelor of Arts Honours degree from Trent University. It was a double honour to receive a degree from a wonderful school and from a great Canadian icon.

DAVID WALLBRIDGE, *via e-mail*

Peter Gzowski was an extraordinary man. He has been described as Mr. Canada, Canada's greatest broadcaster and a national treasure. But to those of us at Trent, and in this community, he was simply "Peter."

Peter's special relationship with Trent began in 1987 when he was awarded an honorary degree for outstanding public service and broadcasting. In 1992, he donated his papers to the Trent University Archives, where his work lives on.

In many ways, it seemed a natural choice to ask him to become chancellor in 1999. When I first called Peter to see if he would let his name stand for chancellor, we discussed three things. First, he wanted the time to talk to his good friend Avie Bennett, chancellor of York University. Second, he thought he'd like an office. If he accepted, he had no intention of being an absentee chancellor – a space on campus would allow him to immerse himself in the life of the university and conduct some of his own research while with us. Third, he informed me that he wasn't a fund-raiser.

The funny thing is that Peter turned out to be an exceptional fund-raiser, lending his name, writing to friends, benefactors and alumni – with excellent results.

Peter's candidacy was enthusiastically supported by our community, and on June 4, 1999, Peter was installed as Trent's eighth chancellor. I should have known what was coming in his spontaneous character when on that day he led the graduates and audience in a resounding chorus of happy birthday to the president. He was full of surprises. When he accepted the nomination, he told me how honoured he was to follow in the footsteps of such respected friends as Ambassador Mary Simon, W.O. Mitchell and Margaret Laurence. He was proud to be part of that history.

Peter truly embraced his role as chancellor, especially convocation. Convocations are unique among the milestones of students' lives, because they celebrate significant accomplishments while anticipating the future. Wind, rain or shine, there is no doubt that Peter made a difference to every Trent student who walked across that outdoor podium.

Each convocation, Peter hosted a luncheon between the morning and afternoon ceremonies for special guests and •

their families. At the 2001 convocation, Ernie Coombs, beloved to Canadians and especially children, was awarded an honorary degree.

Peter was less mobile at that time so we arranged for a car and driver to chauffeur him around campus. Calling it a car and driver might be stretching the truth. Actually, the car was a golf cart and the driver was Roz Taylor, a Trent staff member who worked closely with him.

As Peter returned to the golf cart after the morning convocation, he informed Roz he wanted to go see his good friend Ernie Coombs. Roz was happy to comply, and off they went, chatting with people they ran into along the way. Once they found Ernie, Peter said to Roz, "I'd like to share a glass of wine with Ernie (pause) but don't tell Gill."

Roz was reluctant to comply, but there was no arguing with the chancellor so she brought him a glass. Meanwhile Roz, worrying about his health and his afternoon speech, had diluted the wine with Perrier. A short while later, as Peter went to rest and have a bite to eat, he requested a second glass of wine and added, "This time, Roz (pause), don't water it down!"

That was genuine Peter – sharp to the end.

BONNIE PATTERSON, *Peterborough, Ontario*

I am a retired Trent employee. For many years I worked on grounds maintenance. I, like many other people in Canada, came to know Peter through listening to *Morningside*. One day I was searching for a station, and a student who was working with me suggested that we tune in to CBC. Lo and behold it was Peter's *Morningside* that was on, and from that day forward I became an avid listener. I am sure Trent paid me for a few hours that were spent listening to Peter Gzowski instead of working. (I can only say this because I am retired now.) I found it was his style of interviewing that made him so special. Listeners felt they were right there in the same room with Peter and his guest. He appealed to all ages and all walks of life.

I don't think Trent could have made a better choice for a chancellor than Peter. The day of his installation he made a wonderful speech. It was very hot that graduation day. Peter finished up his speech, then said that he had talked enough and that we should all go down by the river and enjoy a beer. Peter was always thinking of the comfort of his listeners.

The first time I met Peter was at the first Chancellor's Dialogue a couple of years ago. I told him that as a listener he was my hero at CBC. He responded that we, the listeners, were his heroes. And Peter, you will always be my hero.

GENE MCKEIVER, *Peterborough, Ontario*

I was very proud to graduate from Trent University. The day before convocation, I visited my grandpa in the hospital. When he heard that Peter Gzowski would be conferring my degree, he was very excited and asked me to pass on a message for him. Sadly, when I got to the point of shaking Peter's hand, I froze and forgot to give him Grandpa's message.

On June 3, 2001, Grandpa died. I felt terrible that I was unable to fulfil his last request to me. I sent Peter a letter to tell him my grandpa's message but I'm sure he did not get a chance to read it.

My grandpa's message: "Tell Peter that I believe he is the second greatest Canadian . . . after myself!"

MARGIE DAVENPORT, *via e-mail*

When I graduated, I was lucky enough to be handed the degree I'd worked so hard for from the man himself. At the time I was struck by the almost ironic appropriateness of it. I don't believe I have a single memory without Peter's voice somewhere in the background. In fact, one of my earliest memories is of driving through the Rockies with my mother listening to Peter on the radio. I thought it apropos that as my childhood began to end at graduation, he was a part of it.

JONI BRUNTON, *Stouffville, Ontario*

I met Peter Gzowski years ago at the Margaret Laurence Tribute at Trent. A friend of mine had come from Montreal for the occasion. An avid radio fan, she spent the first part of the evening trying to locate Peter in the crowd, not quite sure what he looked like. Finally I told her to shut her eyes and listen. She found him immediately.

LEISHA LeCOUVIE, *Montreal*

Peter gave us a sense of a life being lived to the fullest, as well as of our possibilities to do the same. He loved to point out the many frontiers that life and this country present to inquiring minds and spirits. Trent helped me understand this in my youth; Peter Gzowski helped to expand on this in my adult years.

DEBORAH VAN WYCK, *Montreal*

There once was a great man named Peter
who was a national icon and leader.
He led me to advocate for literacy and laughter,
which we all know he'll continue to inspire many others to do
even in the hereafter.

At last year's convocation you said, "All of you that have mums graduating this year yell out, 'Way to go, Mum.' I was so looking forward to hearing you say that this year when I graduate. I know I will be able to hear you, with your broadcaster voice, speaking those words all the way from Heaven.

KATHIE M. LEECE, *via e-mail*

"The best radio writing (to my ear, anyway) doesn't sound like writing at all. I read my own circumlocutory prose with some ease, for example, because I also talk like that. I put *rhythms* in – long sentence, short sentence – and leave spaces for breathing or changing tone. But I try to type it out so I can read it as if I *hadn't* typed it out. . . . The principle is simply to write for the ear, in conversational language, as opposed to journalese. . . . There's only one listener. . . . People may watch television in groups but they listen to the radio alone: in the kitchen, car, bathroom, etc. That makes radio very intimate, a telephone."

PETER GZOWSKI, *from an undated memo addressed*
to his Morningside *staff*

Peter Gzowski began an association with the university in 1987 upon receiving a Doctor of Laws degree at the fall convocation. Four years later, he donated his papers to Trent and went on to become chancellor in 1999. His was a familiar face on campus, and word would spread quickly that Peter was here. He was apt to approach anyone walking by and ask for their views and opinions on any matter. Peter was like that: interested, very sharp (and ready to trip you up!), and friendly.

Peter wrote to President John Stubbs in October 1991, discussing the disposition of his papers. He referred to his offer to donate them to the university as stemming from "my affinity for what Trent has come to stand for." The university quickly assured him that his papers were not only "worth keeping," but would provide a research resource of inestimable value for decades to come. In 1992, the first of five separate lots of the Gzowski papers arrived at Trent University Archives. Totalling over thirteen metres (forty-three feet), they include correspondence, manuscripts, publishing records, newspaper clippings, photographs and interview tapes.

For many years, people across Canada tuned in to CBC's *Morningside* to listen to a person for whom, judging by their warm and personal letters to the host, they felt a deep affinity and affection. They would follow their "Dear Peter" salutation with an apology for addressing him with such familiarity. We suspect that Peter was quite amused at the various spellings of his last name, as hundreds of bizarre spellings were forwarded to us with his papers, cut from their envelopes.

The Gzowski papers chronicle every aspect of Canadian culture from 1955 to 1999, debating issues, offering opinions and sharing confidences. From abortion, to euthanasia, to sports, to politics, to the arts – a thousand subjects were, at one time or another, debated with passion and heartfelt fervour by ordinary citizens who found a respectful listener in

Ready for a trip North.

The Honourable Stephen Kakfwi, Minister of Education,
requests the pleasure of your company
at a dinner in honour of
The Peter Gzowski
Invitational Golf Tournament for Literacy
Sunday, April 8, 1990
Caribou room, Yellowknife Inn

Reception: 6:00 p.m.	*Regrets only*
(Cash bar)	*Lynn Fogwill*
Dinner: 7:00 p.m.	*Res:*
Dress: Casual	*Off:*

From PG's bulletin board, 1990.

Two PGI scenes: left, absorbing some golf tips from Frank McKenna,
Mactaquac, New Brunswick; right, reviewing his script before the
show at the Red Barn.

Photo courtesy of Peter Bregg, Maclean's

L'INVITATION DE

P ETER G ZOWSKI'S I NVITATIONAL

GOLF TOURNAMENTS IN AID OF CANADIAN LITERACY

P G I

October 5, 1993

Dear Laura and Linda and Sally and Mark,
And Darrel and Willie and Richard and Clark,
And Shelley and Shelley and Chris and Christine,
And Ray, George, Lynne, Carolyn -- all of the team
That Jenny now chairs on an interim plan --
(With some help at the office of Linzey, Joanne):

Just thought I would tell you ere winter sets in
That of all of the meetings where I've ever been
Last week's was the best. But that's easy to say
Since while you guys were working, I got to play.
(Could have golfed if I'd wanted, with Sheila and Kevin,
and should have, I guess, on a day made in heaven),
But...it's not that I wanted no more of the same,
It's just that...well, YOU know - you've seen my game.

So now I am hist'ry - tournament-free.
The movement continues: PGIs sans PG.
(Except for the Briars and NWT.)
It's just what I wanted. I'm pleased as a pea.
You did wonders, scaled mountains, conquered the sea,
And your future looms bright in the years without me.

I'll share in your triumphs, if you all don't mind.
(Hey, Sally, I'm talking like one of your kind.)
But still as I watch from afar what you do,
There'll be one note of sadness: I'm going to miss YOU.

Thanks.

PG

PG says goodbye to the PGIs – of course, by fax.

Peter Gzowski, soon to be Chancellor of Trent University, and Avie Bennett, Chairman of M&S and Chancellor of York University.

PG is gowned for his installation as Chancellor of Trent University, 1999.

Robert Fulford, Ph.D.,
and Peter Gzowski, Ph.D.,
honoris causa, at the
University of Toronto.

Dr. Gzowski with his family.

Morningside, the finale: while PG was in Moose Jaw, the Toronto crew worked from the studio at the Broadcast Centre.

The post-*Morningside* boat cruise: PG with Patsy Pehleman, Hal Wake, Gloria Bishop and Nicole Bélanger. Susan Reisler missed the photo call. These five served as *Morningside*'s Executive Producers at various times over the show's fifteen years.

PG and Shelley Ambrose on the cruise after the last *Morningside*.

With
his first
granddaughter,
Stephanie.

One of my favourite words for snow—and one of my favourite Inuktitut words—is *natiruviaq*. *Natiruviaq* is the wind blowing very low along the ground. It picks up the loose snow and it moves it along, drops it and picks up some more and keeps moving along, so that when you look on the ground, you see this moving snow constantly going places.

Peter is exactly that to Canada. He is that light breeze that moves from province to province, picking up a piece of Canada and dropping it off at the next province, picking up something else and dropping that off at the next province. Peter is that wind that blows across the country. He is our *natiruviaq*.

—Susan Aglukark, Toronto

Peter Gzowski. The depth and breadth of the national argument between and among Canadians, with Peter as catalyst, was profound.

Peter's career in broadcasting, as a journalist and as an author is well documented in the Gzowski papers. An idea of the extent and value of the papers will be obvious from the inventories we have prepared for these papers. Detailed descriptions are available on our web site: http://www.trentu.ca/library/archives/titles.htm. Scroll down to "Gzowski."

These records are permanently preserved and available to any person who is interested in Canadian lives lived, fears met and hopes sustained through shared experiences revealed in conversations with Peter Gzowski.

JODI AOKI AND BERNADETTE DODGE, *Peterborough, Ontario*

from the Trent University Calendar:
Peter Gzowski Northern Scholarship
This scholarship was established by the law firm Heenan Blaikie and by his friends across Canada, to honour the late Peter Gzowski, the eighth Chancellor of Trent University. This scholarship has a focus on students from the north and those studying northern issues.

Requiem

Peter was my big cousin. My earliest memories are from Betlyn, our family cottage on the south shore of Lake Simcoe. Betlyn – the name is derived from the names of our aunt Beth and my mother (Peter's aunt) Jocelyn – was presided over by our grandparents, Vera and Harold Gzowski. As I guess is the case with most grandparents, we called them something quite different. To the adults Harold was "The Colonel" (he was a colonel in the Engineers during World War One), but to all of Peter's and my generation he was Dan Dan and Vera was Danny. They were incredible people. The Colonel was an honest, proud, handsome and very traditional man. Vera, had she been born into Peter's and my generation, I am sure would have, like her eldest grandchild, distinguished herself. She was a talented photographer, a wonderful storyteller, but more than that she truly was a saint. The best listener and sincerest consoler, you always felt better and reassured spiritually after time spent with Danny. Some of the gifts were more tangible, like Ridley tuition.

At Betlyn my brother Patrick and I would occupy the bedroom that had been Peter's, and my bed, which had been his, was against the thin wall to the dining room. I remember many times recalling with Peter the fact that you could hear all the adult conversations, and that in our collective memories there was never a serious profanity nor a harsh or vindictive word spoken. The patter was above all civil, but also witty, informed and insightful. Save for occasionally knowing what you were getting for your birthday prematurely, those eaves-dropped insights into the adult world, I am sure, helped shape both Peter's and my vision of how things can and should be.

Having an older cousin meant having someone in your life who had already blazed the trails you would soon ride. I remember several times being consoled about the social agony of adolescent acne. It was a lifesaver to have someone of the stature of your cool older cousin put the "pimple problem" in perspective. Without ever attempting to dismiss its devastating impact, he always left me believing there was light at the end of the tunnel and that this was not a terminal problem. In matters of the heart, Peter was strategically placed in age halfway between my dad and me. It was perfect. His advice was contemporary and hip; I could even brag a bit. And when he would confide in me I felt so mature, "with it" – a man. As I look back, what characterized his counsel was the perspective and the pragmatic wisdom.

My earliest memories are of someone who could, bare-handed, catch a golf ball thrown at him with all my might. Peter would take me for canoe jaunts into Sutton and could swim across the river and back with ease. This was the family test one needed to pass before being allowed to go out in the canoe alone. One of the neighbours swam to Georgina Island and Peter, upon hearing this, dismissed the feat as easy. He dived in and using the "Australian Crawl," as my grandmother noted, headed off towards the island. He veered to the right and hit dry land at the Mossington pier about three hundred yards away – but it was a great stunt!

Even after I reached an age that should signal adulthood and maturity, Peter was always more worldly and wiser than I. Many times I would be on a rant about an arrogant broadcaster, overrated architect or corrupt politician and Peter, after letting me get to the point of repetition, would interject with some insight that would put things in a different, fairer light, where there were shades of grey, mitigating circumstances and always compassion and humanity. At these times I wasn't always afforded the gentle forgiving treatment reserved for the chilli sauce maker in Gander.

In my adult relationship with my famous cousin, the contrast and similarity between the public and private Peter were always fascinating. Once, around a fall fire at Betlyn, the subject had turned to unions and the destructive way we negotiate our terms and conditions of employment. After many of us had had our turn on the soapbox, Peter let go with a most insightful, revealing analysis (I truly wish I could have recorded it). There was just family, no feelings to spare, this was Peter with some strongly held, brilliantly developed thoughts, not Captain Canada, the consummate interviewer. It was great – precision of language, profundity, balanced arguments sprinkled with historical references – and then it was on to cards and darts. Those were the best of times.

At my daughter's wedding, as he welcomed Ken to our family, Peter characterized Stacey as the princess of Betlyn and Mary, my wife, as the queen. Mary always made monumental efforts to get Peter's five wonderful, but hard to assemble, children together for special occasions. My mum's birthday in midsummer was the one where she experienced the most success. Those were great times, with Peter playing games with his granddaughters Stephanie and Samantha on the same lawn he and I played catch with golf balls all those years ago.

Peter and I were a good fit in another way. He was forever a bit of a nomad, and I had declared myself a cabinetmaker and architectural designer. I do hope after a couple of decades my proclamation is a little closer to being accurate. Over the years we have conspired on many renovations and custom bits of furniture. Peter was impetuous and invariably wanted things finished before the PGI at the Briars for that year. I, on the other hand, insisted on a participatory design process. I believe we moved each other towards the centre over the years, although the concept of finishing a project is still one I am working to grasp.

For his birthday I built Peter a desk of solid mahogany. The lumber I ordered came in a single board, twenty-four inches wide by three inches deep by over thirty-eight feet long. When I attempted to engage him in a philosophical discourse on the spirit of the material, he raised his hand and said, "Okay – I get it – cut the tree down and chip away all the stuff that doesn't look like a desk."

During one of our many renovation projects, I had a disagreement with one of the team we were collaborating with. It seemed to me the best thing was for me to withdraw – there would be other projects and I didn't want to put Peter in the position of aesthetic mediator. When I arrived to deliver the news to Peter and Gill, they were ready for me. The gist of what Peter said was that this was just a fix-up and that we would be spending many, many years sitting around this table, and he didn't want to have old Jack whining about some interior details. As it turned out there were not nearly enough of those years.

JACK MADDEN, *Sutton, Ontario*

Well, I have spent most of the week sitting in my office staring at the walls. It was a week of waiting. You want to know how I feel today, now that the waiting is over, I feel sad and I feel lonely. That's how I feel.

You want to know what I think? I think Peter Gzowski had a remarkable career. I think he did great work. Somewhere, a long time ago, Peter decided it was his mission to uncover the best of Canada, the people and the places, to seek them out and introduce them to the rest of us.

Because he decided this was important work, and because he was so good at it, we believed it was important work, too. And we went along for the ride.

That's not all I think. I think that somewhere along the way, Peter became what he was looking for. He became a part of the best of Canada.

He was the best of CBC Radio, that's for sure.

He was a sort of quilt maker. The individual parts of his quilt were often quite ordinary. Some of the moments, of course, were extra-special – the first interview with Elly Danica, the Red River Rally, to name two – but mostly, like any quilter worth his or her salt, he worked with scraps. It was only when you stepped back and looked at the overall effect that you realized the grandeur of his creation.

That's what I think.

You want to know what he was like. He was a bundle of contradictions. He wasn't the guy you thought you knew from the radio. And he was the guy you knew from the radio.

If you didn't know him, and you met him, you might have been disappointed. You might have thought he was chilly and stand-offish. He wasn't chilly and stand-offish. He just acted that way sometimes. People say he was shy. I think he was more private than shy. I think there is a difference.

He was certainly complicated.

He was a man who dealt in the realm of ideas. But he was driven to ideas by instinct and emotion. He was the Canadian nationalist who more than anything wanted to have written for the *New Yorker* magazine.

He was a serious person who liked to play games. Especially if they involved words.

He was sloppy about his clothes and meticulous about his grammar. On New Year's Eve, he provoked one of the guests he had invited to dinner to search through a stack of reference books in an effort to determine whether it was more Canadian to say railroad or railway.

He was more a journalist than a gentleman.

He was thoughtful and he was selfish.

His work absorbed him. He noticed everything. Except the world around him. One day his friend Peter Sibbald Brown went to his cottage at Lake Simcoe. You didn't knock on the door up there, you just wandered in, and Peter Sibbald Brown did that and found the cottage filled with smoke. Coughing, eye-stinging smoke, and he thought, even Gzowski couldn't generate this much smoke. He put his hands over his eyes and staggered in and found a log had tumbled out of the fireplace and was smouldering on the hardwood floor.

Gzowski was sitting at his computer in the little alcove where he worked. He had noticed the smoke. But his off-hand response was to crack the window open about a quarter of an inch.

You want to know how I'll remember him? I'll remember him sitting across from me in a radio studio with his head down. I'll remember him ignoring me while he scribbled a last-minute note onto a script with a black marker. I'll remember him rewriting intros fifteen seconds before we went to air.

And I'll remember him looking up at me with a mischievous smile. He did that on the radio and he did that in his
home. Pleased as punch because he found a question that
would shift the spotlight away from him. His mission was to
make others shine brighter. He seemed to bring out the best in
those he was with.

STUART MCLEAN, *Toronto*

Let me say up front, I find it very difficult to write anything
about Peter Gzowski. It's hard to describe how much I miss
him now, never mind how much I will miss him down the road.
I miss the comforting sound of his voice in the morning,
although there was always the chance his "best of" would calm
the airwaves later in the day.

I am very sad that I didn't have the chance to say goodbye
before he ventured on a new journey. But then something very
strange happened. I heard wonderful voices singing, poetry
recited, friends laughing . . . and finally a conversation between
Peter and W.O. Mitchell. I felt myself smiling at the power of
love and what Peter had done for me and everyone else who
was blessed to have known him.

TOM JACKSON, *Calgary*

Like so many of us, for years I met many, indeed most, of our
public figures through Peter. Living a forty-minute round trip
from the nearest *Globe and Mail*, I probably learned more
about the off-island world from Gzowski interviews than from
any other source. The Free Trade debate, Meech Lake, the

Gulf War – it was *Morningside*, not the *National* or the *Journal* or the *Globe*, that provided the full spectrum of opinions. It was Peter who moderated our civic life.

That was my public relationship with Peter Gzowski, and I expect it influenced me about as much as my personal relationship with him, which is to say, profoundly. As editor of the *Star Weekly*, Peter published my first piece of professional writing, a reminiscence of my high-school years, written at the ripe old age of twenty-two. When he moved on to edit *Maclean's*, he asked me to write again . . . and again, until at twenty-four I had a monthly column. (We called it "Token Radical.") Peter fixed me up with Harry Bruce as my editor. I was probably too young and full of myself to appreciate my good fortune. But, thereby, I learned my trade. Then Peter got fired.

A year or two passed until, one August afternoon (it could have been 1972), I stopped in at Peter's Toronto Island house. In those days I used to take my banjo (and probably a joint) and find an empty corner of Snake Island and strum away a few hours. On this occasion I said to Peter, "Hey, I've got a new song." I played him "Daddy Was a Ballplayer." He said he was about to begin hosting a new CBC morning radio program and why didn't we – Stringband was in its infancy – sing it on the show. I remember they didn't have the budget to pay all three of us union scale, so Marie-Lynn and I played, and Gerry the fiddler stayed home. We may even have been *This Country in the Morning*'s first musical guests.

As would be the case for thousands of musicians over the following decades, our audience suddenly shifted from local to national. From there it was all roses, limos, the bright lights and the big bucks of the folk singer's life.

Then, in the early eighties, I agreed to emcee the Vancouver Folk Music Festival, a daunting task, akin to being the

intermission pianist at a strip show. I knew Peter had hosted
the Winnipeg Folk Festival, so I called him for his advice.
"Don't tell jokes," he said. I promised I wouldn't. Then he
said, "It's the same as anything else. Just listen. If you listen
you'll know what to do."

BOB BOSSIN, *Gabriola Island, British Columbia*

I've been thinking lately about the time I spent in the presence
of Peter Gzowski. Whether speaking to him on the radio or
taking part in the cross-country sing-alongs he loved so much,
or even just hanging around backstage at the Red Barn or the
Music Hall here in Toronto, those encounters were very
meaningful to me. I felt a strong connection to him, as did a
great many others. Peter loved music and he loved musicians.
He was endlessly curious about how it all worked and not
afraid to show emotion when something moved him – the
timbre of a voice, a certain lyric. I remember with great fondness his shyness and his sweetness and how he always made a
girl from Bible Hill, Nova Scotia, feel very much appreciated
and very special.

CINDY CHURCH, *Toronto*

Peter and I first met at a folk festival out west, sometime back
in the seventies. We took to each other immediately and
walked around all day eating ice cream. We were friends from
then on.

There are not many things that will make a musician get
up very early in the morning. Peter was one.

Let us all raise our glasses in toast
To the man who was Canada's Host.
Somehow, somewhere out there
He is still on the air
And we'll all meet again, ghost-to-ghost.

The comforting sound of Peter's voice will always be just over my shoulder.

JOAN BESEN, *Toronto*

Peter came to Ridley College as Peter Brown. It doesn't matter what the reasons were for this, but within a short time he became Peter Gzowski. His fame as a linguist had not penetrated all of his colleagues and hence there was speculation that his choice of a name, which had a silent G in front of the Z, must have arisen from some kind of oversight. It soon became evident, however, that Peter wished to have his birth name returned. He was fiercely proud of that name, fiercely proud of his Polish heritage, fiercely proud of his great-great-grandfather, Sir Casimir Stanislaus Gzowski, whose statue resides in Toronto to this day as a legacy of his community contributions, and fiercely proud of his wonderful grandparents, who were intent on him experiencing as much benefit as possible from an educational opportunity.

This adherence to his roots is reflected in his ability to speak proudly and sincerely with Canadians in every walk of life – victims of sexual assault, plumbers, lawyers, carpenters, bread bakers and so on. It is this adherence to his roots and his willingness to stand up and be counted that has endeared him to all Canadians.

JOHN GIRVIN, *London*

Dear Monsieur Gzowski,

I know you used to read all of the letters that were sent to you at the CBC. You are probably reading this one. Many people have thanked you for having given them, over the years, intelligent radio for their mornings. You were interested in all of the voices of Canada. Because you knew how to listen so well, the whole country perked up its ears. Your work is well known. In Australia, for example, a radio journalist told me that after he heard you, he decided to change his way of going about his own work. Today, as National Librarian of Canada, I want to thank you so much for your efforts to fight a terrible misery in our society – illiteracy. I also want to thank you for promoting Canadian literature. You were a pioneer in this area and you supported the work of the other pioneers – our poets, our novelists and our publishers.

Finally, I would like to thank you personally for having invited me onto your show many times. I think you were a little timid, and I am a bit shy. But, from one show to the next, we developed an "electronic friendship," as we agreed to call it. Because, when there wasn't a microphone between us, it was a little more difficult to have a conversation. I have some great memories: Like the day in your office, where, in spite of the no-smoking rules, you were immersed in smoke, because your little machine that was supposed to eat up the smoke wasn't powerful enough. And the time you invited me on your show with Maurice Richard and you presented my scrapbook to The Rocket and his to me. And because twenty-five years ago, you presented my little novel *The Hockey Sweater* on your show, I am still autographing this little book for kids who are not even born yet.

Merci, Monsieur Gzowski.

ROCH CARRIER, *Ottawa*

This spring, I visited the CBC's web site, where my father's virtual memorial still lives. This was my first visit. (I haven't yet been able to look at the mass of clippings that my love Mary saved for me in the weeks after my father's death.) Among other things, this excellent multimedia tribute offered sound clips of great moments from *Morningside*. Among them was my father's show-opening essay for the day Ben Johnson was stripped of his Olympic gold medal. I was surprised and pleased to see it there. Somehow, I thought I was the only person to remember that moment.

To a certain extent, my father was always a shared commodity to me. My parents separated when I was twelve. From then on, I had irregularly scheduled, regular fatherly visits with him, but we would never spend more than a few days together at one stretch. My father was a very busy man. We'd talk on the phone occasionally, but the famous broadcaster was famously bad on the phone. Among my siblings and me, his short, gruff calls were a running joke and not to be taken personally. He was who he was. So for the rest of the time, I was like all of his listeners and readers, a passive, appreciative audience of his work. But I was also able to meet my father's intellect in a way few people whose parents aren't public figures do. I was and am proud of him. And unlike other fans' relationships with their fathers, when mine was at work, if I was mad at him I could tell him to shut up and turn him off anytime I wanted to. But I usually didn't. Instead, I would procrastinate beginning my day and listen to just one more item. . . .

The essay he wrote and performed about Ben Johnson is a gem. He reads like he's not reading, and he wrote like he wasn't writing. In less than two minutes, he acutely expressed my Canadian's disappointment with the news and then miraculously swung my sympathy onto Ben Johnson's side. It was so good I don't know how I could have ever thought it wasn't

every fan's *Morningside* favourite. But I did. When I saw it
on the CBC web site, reality crashed in. I had experienced his
work the way everyone who didn't work on his shows did,
thinking it was just for them, that we had a special relationship.
With his work, we didn't. It was made for everyone to share. I
silently thanked whoever on that venerable team chose to offer
us the Ben Johnson essay, then I listened to it and cried. I cried
then like I haven't cried since the week he died.

A little while later, after wringing out my shirt, I thought
about the plethora of recordings that exist of my father's
thoughts and words. I realized it was the sound of his voice
that made me emotional, making me think for a moment that
he was still alive, and then having to remember the sad truth.
He ain't coming back, as they say in the movies. But soon I
came to the conclusion that I was lucky, that the recordings,
and all his books, will help keep him alive for me. This then
may be the payoff for all those years of sharing my father with
his fans: that even after his death, a huge part of him is and
always will be available to me.

MICK GZOWSKI, *Toronto*

It was the damned cigarettes, of course, that killed Peter
Gzowski before his time. Addiction to nicotine, and to the
comfort and company and instant gratification of smoking,
was a demon we shared. In the years when he was a fellow
columnist at the *Star* and would emerge from his office to
share column-writing perplexities, we always spoke over our
mutual wreaths of smoke.

Every time we talked, he lamented his unwilling exile from
CBC Radio, fretting about how to get back on the air after his
debacle on television. He enlisted me in one such effort to

regain a toehold at the Mother Corp. Together, we did a daily, five-minute debate for the drive-home show about hockey, or the Soviet Union, or men and women – and we always managed to hoke up some joshing mock outrage or friendly disagreement with each other.

This was at a time when I was writing five columns a week and bringing up three children under the age of twelve, without much help either at the office or home. No wonder I needed those cigarettes to keep me going.

Peter has written about his cigarette habit more eloquently, and with less self-pity or self-justification, than anyone else I know. When I read his marvellously fluent, funny and revealing chapter, "How to Quit Smoking in Fifty Years or Less," in last year's book *Addicted*, I was struck by Peter's unstated but terrible yearning, loss and love for his glamorous mother, who died at thirty-nine. When she learned that her son had started smoking, she offered him one of her own. "I think she was more amused than angry," Peter recalled, and "maybe even secretly pleased that I had taken another step on the road to manhood."

Is it any wonder that, years and thousands of cigarettes later, when smoking had become so firmly a part of Peter's identity, he didn't succeed in dozens of efforts to quit because, as he admitted, "my heart wasn't in it"?

The causes of addiction are a terrible tangle. Like Peter, I started to smoke at twelve. A fake tough swagger took me through an uncomfortable adolescence. The first time I quit, at forty, I was astonished by the emotional turmoil, the sharp stab of loss that jabbed me into sudden tears at the memory of my long-dead and unmourned father, with whom I shared practically nothing except our reliance on cigarettes.

What nobody seems to talk about is how much false energy you get from cigarettes. Only while I smoked could I work eighteen hours a day, flat out. Considering Peter's gruelling schedule and the level of his productivity, I'm not surprised he clung to the nicotine that pumped him through his days. For a while, after Peter had joyfully returned to the CBC to launch *This Country in the Morning*, I did weekly "Ontario Reports" with Tory Hugh Segal – both Peter and I filling up the squalid tin ashtray, using Hugh's moments on air to cover our microphones and cough. Then, for a dozen or more years, I was part of the program's children's book panel, so I was still there (and habit-free) when the new anti-smoking rules drove Peter out on to the sidewalk during the station breaks.

In his last couple of years on the CBC, I was surprised to learn that we also shared the same caring family doctor, and that he had given her permission to enlist me as one of his quit-smoking advisers. It didn't work, of course. His "heart wasn't in it." Like most smokers, he was ashamed, guilty, disgusted, angry with himself – and frightened to give it up.

If you're still smoking, think about the price that everyone pays for any smoker's habit. For the smoker, and for everyone left behind, the price is, eventually, an agony.

MICHELE LANDSBERG, *Toronto*

I had a privileged place in Peter's life as his family doctor. When I was asked to contribute to this book, I hesitated because of patient confidentiality, wondering what Peter would want me to say. Though he liked to kibitz with my secretary and the occasional fan he met in the elevator on his way to the office, like many public personalities, Peter valued his privacy. In our waiting room he would sit somewhat anonymously while those around him buried their heads in their magazines. Did they not know who he was or were they simply being good Canadians by ignoring him? In the end, I decided I could comment on the subjects Peter himself had shared publicly and offer my perspective on the partnership we had.

Peter's most public health issue was his well-known struggle with smoking, which eventually played a role in ending his life. Over the seven years I was his doctor, we tried various strategies to help Peter give up cigarettes. In helping smokers, I have learned that solutions must be personalized because the habit behaves differently in each person. We'd discuss and try one strategy after another, and inevitably Peter would come back contrite, confessing what a "bad patient" he was and how sorry he felt for me. That led to long debates about the difference between blame and responsibility. I didn't have much patience for self-flagellation, appreciating that, even in its sincerity, beating up on oneself was not the route to changing an entrenched behaviour. I was there to support him when he could face the internal demons that contributed to his dependency and to find the very best people to help him do that.

We were very frank with one another. At one point I let him know the risks of smoking while wearing a nicotine patch. The next time his eyes twinkled as he admitted to me that now when he wanted a cigarette he simply took the patch off.

As Peter has written elsewhere, everything he did was somehow tied to smoking. To quit would be physically and psychologically stressful, we both knew, and so we agreed that the ideal time to quit was when Peter had some "down time." Except that never was going to happen. Each time he'd plan for it there'd be another commitment; first a taxing schedule at *Morningside*, and later, after he left morning radio, a speaking engagement, a trip north, a book tour, one awards ceremony after another – it went on and on. That's when we came up with the idea that in order to quit he needed time out of his life. His tobacco addiction was formidable and worthy of the kind of attention a residential program could offer. He agreed to enter a treatment program but was wary about doing any group work. "Hello, my name is Peter and I'm addicted to nicotine." He'd mock and shake his head.

I phoned ahead. Protective of him, I warned the staff physician that he was only willing to do individualized work. I think the doctor humoured me, and shortly after Peter's admission convinced him to try the group. In fact, Peter's insatiable curiosity and interest in people and their stories overrode his need for privacy. He became enthralled with the other residents and formed close connections to some of the participants, enjoying the opportunity to reach out and help some of them.

He was successful. Peter defeated a ravaging fifty-year-plus addiction. He was buoyant at being able to accomplish this feat. Whatever happened later, with his decreasing lung function, he was so grateful that he wouldn't die still smoking.

As time went on and his breathing capacity dwindled, he enrolled in a respiratory rehabilitation program where again he responded to competent, caring people who gave him hope and a structured program to improve his breathing. "The breathing academy" was his affectionate term for West Park Health Centre, run by Dr. Roger Goldstein and his superb staff.

Peter has written about his admiration for the Canadian health care system. With the exception of one nurse who, during an earlier hospital stay, entered his room on roller skates to offer him a cigarette, he had nothing but praise for his team of specialists, nurses, physiotherapists and respiratory therapists. He referred to me as the captain of his team, and I did my best to live up to the faith he had in me. He coped with being dependent on oxygen by "coming out" publicly about his addiction and becoming an advocate for the work of the Lung Association. We talked openly about everything from the option of lung transplantation to the possibility of living on a mechanical respirator. Peter did not want any of that. As with any of my patients, I saw my role as enhancing his quality of life. We'd check in regularly between visits by phone, or when necessary, I would make a house call. I vetoed any investigation that would not change the outcome and only make him uncomfortable. Wherever I could, in consultation with his specialists, I tried to clarify and simplify his medications. Peter could not keep all those drugs straight, referring to them as the blue ones and the red ones, so I and the staff at West Park wrote out explicit instructions for him. In fact he was scheduled to go back to the breathing academy the week his breathing deteriorated.

My consolation is that until shortly before his death, Peter could still do some of the things that gave him pleasure. An impassioned Scrabble player, he won a fierce competition three weeks before he died. He continued to write his column for the *Globe and Mail*. With assistance, he was able to attend to his duties as chancellor at Trent University. Because of the way we were able to work together, and with the support of those closest to him, Peter was spared the frantic emergency room visits, long waits, hospital admissions and readmissions so common for people with chronic obstructive lung disease. He had the good fortune to choose how he wanted to die and a loving family to support his wishes.

My feeling for Peter had little to do with his celebrity status and everything to do with the kind of person he was. Courteous, and appreciative of anything that was done for him, he was not, contrary to his belief, a demanding patient. He would lean forward, concentrating as if conducting an interview, and try to get inside my head, eager to grasp more of me than my mere words. We'd argue. We'd laugh. The technical terms for the kind of bond we developed in our therapeutic alliance are transference and counter-transference. We fell in love with one another, not in any romantic sense, but in the recognition we were sharing a most intimate journey with another human being. I feel blessed for having been able to make that journey with Peter.

PAULINE PARISER, *Toronto*

We Are Sorry for Our Loss

So now we can't tune in to hear the familiar stutter-stammer
    of your rumpled voice
a voice that erased the noise – that static – that happens over
    airwaves
when lines are down, connections lost.
That voice that hugged us in and hushed the racket and the
    rattle
of ourselves inside our separate shells.
And so, we are sorry for our loss

Now we have no excuse to linger over
one more cuppa coffee with you but must:
    get on with all our days, do things like:
    hang out that other load of laundry, finish up
        the vacuuming,
    get back to making notes for tomorrow's big negotiation,
    pound in a few more nails on the houses we are building,
    pick up another fare before our shift is through
    grow the oregano, herd the sheep, carve that Inukshuk
    take off for outer space

We're sorry for the loss
of all those words that no voice will ever sing the same:
words that were your favourites like:

Pangnirtung, Tuktoyaktuk, Palatuk, Inuvik, Iqaluit,
    Nunavut,

Before you said them? Only words.
Black dots on a piece of paper
called a map of a country that's called Canada
But afterwards? Dots connected in a zig-zag puzzle
the magnificent enigma of a nation —
of a people and a place.

And now, such sensory deprivation because:
Without being there you took us there
We really smelled that cod by God
    tasted those worms
    traced the scars of some brave survivor beneath our
        fingertips,
    heard the song inside the singer's heart, not just the music,
    held our breath as someone told us how she finally learned
        to read
    & golfed in the snow one first of July
    & drank the water from an iceberg in the Arctic ocean
    & looked directly in the eyes of an Inuit elder.
    & saw the aurora borealis —

We are *so* sorry for our loss

    yet blessed that we can mourn a man who every morning
    listened to our many selves and some might say, our souls

So we'll replay the tapes, the ones still tucked inside our heads,
    our hearts.
Rest that voice, dear friend, but not your ears.
Tune in from time to time, for if you please, sir
we prefer to think that you will always listen as you
    always have
to this maple-leafed polyphony:
our *voices, travelling over airwaves,*
shining forth, as yours did
from sea to sea to sea.

SHEREE FITCH, *River John, Nova Scotia*

It was a few minutes after midnight on January 1, 2002. The bells had rung in the new year.

It had become a tradition to spend New Year's Eve with Pete and Gill, though we had missed last year because they were away in the tropics. So it felt doubly good for Denise and me to be at the new Gzowski/Howard house with a small group of their close friends.

Our son, Duncan, was having his customary good time riding Pete's chair elevator up and down the basement stairs and channel-surfing on the basement big-screen TV while the rest of us socialized upstairs.

I was very impressed to note that not only did Peter have a clean new sweater on, he was wearing slacks with a crease in them. I complimented him on how neat and pretty he looked, especially compared to his usual rumpled standards.

Peter was in a great humour. I sat for a while at the dining room table with Stuart McLean and Sheila O'Brien, listening to him talk animatedly about how rewarding he found being chancellor at Trent University, talking about the relationships he had developed with students. He talked enthusiastically about the column he was working on for the *Globe*. He was engaged and animated and I recollect sitting there taking it in and wondering at how solid and how smart he was. He seemed full of energy and possibility.

Of course, he was also sitting with nasal canula connecting him to an oxygen machine and drinking mineral water. I had stopped noticing that by now. You accept your friends for how they are.

Denise and I had brought along a whole bunch of giant sparklers and a big jug of pretty good Champagne, and when the clock struck midnight, everybody whooped it up and got a glass of bubbly, then went out on the deck and lit the sparklers, writing our names in the air in the darkness, making happy noises.

Of course, Peter couldn't come out and do that. He was on pure oxygen, which mixes poorly with open flame.

I turned to look through the sliding patio doors and there was Pete, standing by the dining room table, peering through his glasses at the rest of us, holding on to his virtuous glass of mineral water. I looked at him and for a second I thought, "You poor bastard!"

Then, as if he read my mind, he stood up a little straighter, lifted one hand and pretended to write his name in the air with an imaginary sparkler. It was such a sweet and childlike pantomime that it made me laugh.

I didn't know this night was going to be the last chance I would have to talk to Peter in this world. Denise and I went to see him in the hospital and to give our arm to Gill if she wanted it. We knew we were there to say goodbye.

In the few days after Peter passed away, I was working on a lyric for a piece of music I had received from a young composer named Stephan Mocchio. We were ostensibly working on something for a new recording artist, a young girl from Cape Breton. I listened to Stephan's beautiful piano piece and began to write a lyric.

Within seconds I realized who I was writing it for.

MURRAY McLAUCHLAN, *Toronto*

Say Goodbye

Wish I could whistle down the northern lights
And send them dancing all across the night
Maybe then
When all the sky was blazing
Maybe then
I'd feel you somewhere
Gazing at a star
And you could feel me too
As I say goodbye to you
It breaks my heart in two
To say goodbye to you

Wish time could turn us back to yesterday
The gods above would look the other way
Maybe then
We still could laugh together
Maybe then
It could be spring forever and a day
But I must face the truth
And say goodbye to you
It breaks my heart in two
To say goodbye to you
Wish I could whistle down the northern lights

And send them dancing all across the night
Maybe then
In my memories for saving
One last time
You're on the hill
Waving from afar
Just one last glance or two
Then I'll say goodbye to you
It breaks my heart in two
To say goodbye to you

Afterword

To Sir, With Love

The first thing he ever said to me was "Why would you want this job if you live in Windsor?"

It was a Saturday morning in 1986 and I was twenty-four years old. I'd been working as a summer intern reporter for the Windsor *Star*. The day before had been my last day, and the staff had taken me to the press club for many, many goodbye drinks. I was packing up and reading the paper when the phone rang. A friend I'd gone to journalism school with, calling to tell me that Stuart McLean, who had been one of our instructors, had told her Peter Gzowski's assistant at CBC Radio's *Morningside* was moving to Australia. After we hung up, I went back to the paper. Right next to my last by-line was an ad – South Shore Books declaring Peter Gzowski would be there that very day, signing books. The store was directly across the street from the office I had to clear out before returning to Toronto and my part-time job at the *Globe and Mail*. My hangover disappeared instantly, and I got my résumé together, jumped on my bike and pedalled to South Shore Books. The line-up of Gzowski fans was out the door and halfway around the block. I grabbed a coffee, thought better and bought two, then joined the line. It took forever to get to the table where he was sitting, and when I did, there were still scores of people clutching books behind me, so I tried to hurry.

"Hello," I said, "my name is Shelley Ambrose. You don't know me but I have heard via Stuart McLean that you are in need of a new assistant and I thought I'd bring down my résumé so you could read it on the train on the way back to Toronto."

He looked at me, striking what would become a familiar pose, peering over his glasses as if he was so near-sighted he had to lower the lenses to look at your face up close. (Months later, I realized the lenses were so filthy he couldn't see through them. He had a habit of pushing them up with four fingers placed directly on the lenses. Years later, I'd take the glasses off his face and give them a good cleaning. He'd put them on and say, "Ah, so that's what you look like.") Then he asked: "Why would you want this job if you live in Windsor?"

"I don' t really live here," I explained, "I'm just here working on a summer contract for the paper. I'm on my way back to Toronto today."

"And I'm not taking the train," he said.

"Oh?" I replied, brilliantly.

"How are *you* getting back?"

"My boyfriend is coming to get me. Why?"

"Well, I'll be done here by one," he said, "but my flight isn't until six-thirty tonight."

"I'd offer you a ride," I said, "but I'm stopping overnight at my grandmother's, in Chatham."

"Chatham?" he said thoughtfully. "It's been a while since I was in Chatham."

I didn't know if that meant he wanted the ride with me and my boyfriend and my hanging plants and suitcases or not. I pushed my envelope with my résumé and clippings across the table and turned to leave.

"Is one of those for me?" he asked, indicating the two coffees still gripped in my hands.

"Um, yes, one of them was going to be," I lied, "but I've waited so long, they're ice cold."

"Oh," he replied, a bit disappointed. The shuffling horde behind me was getting restless, so I made my exit and went across the street to pack my desk. It was Saturday so it was just me and the police radio blaring away. I sat at my desk and pondered. While he hadn't asked me a single normal question, he'd learned a lot in just a few minutes. So had I. I wasn't certain I'd made a very good impression, and I was fairly sure he didn't really want to go to Chatham but he did want to go home earlier. I picked up the phone, called the airline and found out there was a three o'clock flight to Toronto. I finished packing, grabbed a fresh cup of coffee and made my way back to the bookstore. When I got to the front of the line this time, I handed him the coffee and told him, "You are now booked on a three o'clock flight. I didn't cancel your later flight, but at least now you have the option."

He peered at me again, laughed, nodded and said: "We can talk. Can you wait?"

"Of course," I said, and I stepped to the side. In what I would learn was typical Gzowski fashion, his book-signing table was in a state of uncontrolled madness. An overflowing ashtray, books, pens, gifts and notes – he had nowhere for the coffee. I started to tidy up, collecting the gifts, stacking the books, making space. When I waved at someone in line, he once again peered over his glasses at me. I bent down and whispered, "Um, those people next in line are Mr. and Mrs. So-and-So. They were your hosts here in Windsor when you were the guest of honour at a Writers Development Trust dinner last fall."

"Ah," he said, and stood up as they approached, extending his hand and calling them by name.

After the crowd left, he didn't have much time and he spent it explaining he was a difficult person to work with – a perfectionist, a workaholic, a grump – and advised me that I really didn't want this job. It was one of the few times in the next fifteen years that he was wrong.

∾

Weeks later, once I had the job, Peter gave me a single directive: "No bullshitting. Never, ever pretend you know something when you don't. If you don't know something, say 'I don't know.' Then go and find out." I learned many things from Peter over the years, typewriter clacking in the background, a blue haze of tobacco smoke and a healthy measure of irreverence filling the air.

∾

Three years after the meeting in Windsor, we were at the CBC Radio studios on the seventh floor of the magical Chateau Laurier in Ottawa, doing *Morningside* "on remote." Peter was, among other things, interviewing the prime minister. Once the show was over, we gathered our gear and headed down to sit on the steps in front of the hotel to await a taxi to the airport. We sat – smoking, of course – surrounded by a mishmash of luggage, scripts and tapes spilling out of bags. We'd arrived the day before, for a PGI, had "done" the golf tournament and the dinner and festivities afterwards, and Peter had been in the studio since about five a.m. We were tired and cranky. Suddenly the doors burst open and the prime minister and his entourage emerged from the Chateau, having stayed on after the *Morningside* interview to do a local radio spot. A stream of black cars and Jeeps appeared, and a half dozen men talking into their sleeves and looking very serious grabbed the PM, saying, "Morning sir, here sir, there sir, yes sir, no sir," as they escorted him into his car. The entire entourage left the hotel grounds for the six-second drive next door to the House of Commons, leaving us on the steps like a pair of homeless waifs.

Peter snorted and said, "How come no one ever calls *me* sir?"

"I'll call you sir," I said immediately. "From now on I'll call you sir all the time, every day."

"The hell you will! Don't you dare!" he said. And so, of course, I did. Morning sir, yes sir, no sir. All the time, every day.

∽

By the fall of 1989, when Peter's next book appeared, he'd gotten used to the nickname (even though every time someone else heard me call him sir and, thinking it a serious honorific and the proper way to address Peter Gzowski, also began to address him as sir, he winced and threw me a withering look) and, secretly, liked it. Inside my copy of the book, he wrote: "Love Sir[*] – Christmas 1989.
^{**}Peter Gzowski to the rest of the world."

By then, I was his assistant, one of his producers, the national organizer of the PGI golf tournaments and concerts, and assisted in compiling the books and edited and produced for broadcast the piles of correspondence that arrived from what Peter considered to be the smartest people in Canada –

his listeners. Peter was enormously attached to the morning mail. Once he read all the letters, he'd scrawl (practically indecipherable) notes on them before placing the pile on my desk on his way to the studio. Then I'd go through the letters and corresponding notes, separating them into piles: "thanks," "mailbag," "reader," "RFI" (request for information). I'd edit the mailbag letters into packs for Shelagh Rogers and Peter to read on the air. Occasionally, there was a letter that Peter answered right away, and he'd attach his reply, banged out on his ancient typewriter (you wouldn't believe what we went through trying to find replacement ribbons even then), full of mistakes and scrawled on – again unreadable. I'd edit and retype them and send them out.

When he received a letter that really riled him, he'd fire off a hefty reply, admonishing the addressee in no uncertain terms. I'd store these letters in a drawer and show them to him the next day. He always said, "Don't send that, I'll do it again." And he would.

One day after reading an especially tiresome letter, he said, "You know, Stephen Leacock used to keep a file called Letters from Stupid People." So we started a file. It's a testament to how much Peter thought of the people who wrote – and what they wrote – that when *Morningside* ended forever, that file had only about a half-dozen letters in it.

Peter took his cues from his listeners – and from his guests. *Morningside* was live, don't forget – for three exhilarating hours a day, five gruelling days a week. Not everyone understood the nuances and restrictions of live radio. Not even some of the powers-that-be at the CBC. Peter had, shall we say, a love-hate relationship with CBC management. He can be forgiven his ambivalence: Sometimes they didn't quite get what he – we – did all day. Consider the time the phone rang at 10:15 a.m.

and a woman's voice announced, "I'm calling from the Office of the President of the CBC."

"Yes," I said, "good morning."

"The president would like to speak to Mr. Gzowski."

"Certainly," I said, "when?"

"Now," she said, "he's waiting in his office."

Having to explain to the Ottawa office of the president of the Corporation that at 10:15 a.m. Peter was live on the national airwaves, available for any Canadian to hear, just as he had been for a number of years, and quite unable to take a phone call from anyone, was dispiriting, to say the least. But, except for one decidedly pointed remark to interviewer David Macfarlane about a certain "son of a bitch" – for which he apologized later – Peter did not air his grievances publicly. He understood that if we complained too much about the "disconnect" we perceived between those who ran the CBC and those who made and listened to the programs, we'd be cutting off our public-broadcast-loving noses to spite our faces. It was Peter's perspective that if we joined the "nay-sayers," the oft-repeated idea that the CBC should be burned to the ground and rebuilt in a better model might gain momentum. If it ever burned, he knew it would never be built again. Having the CBC – and public broadcasting – exist at all was far more important than anything else. If we wanted change, it had to happen from within.

One of the ways Peter changed public broadcasting forever (although many broadcasters, even some within the CBC, still haven't cottoned on) was not through political means – it was by doing what was second nature to him. He talked every morning to the listener. Singular. He never said, "Some of you may have seen" or "Many of you watched." He didn't think that way, either. Peter would say, "You may have seen" or "If you are one of those who watched." He knew radio was an individual experience. The host and his (or her) guests were in your kitchen in the morning, or in your car, or in your office. I may miss Peter most when I hear a radio host talk as if there are three of me in the room. I yell at the radio, "Hello! It's just me here, by myself, you're talking to me." Or I want to write a letter expressing that "some of me" was truly ticked.

Was that it, then? Was that his secret? Partly, yes. But there was so much more. Peter got up early and did his homework. He wrote his own bills (those words of greeting and a "billboard" of what was coming up on the show that day) every morning, weaving it all together. He read all the books and went to all the places and met all the people. He worked harder than anyone I have ever seen.

∾

I must admit there were times he exasperated me. He would stand behind my chair while I was on the phone – which was always – and, trying to get my attention, would jingle the change in his pocket until I turned, glared at him, covered the receiver with my hand and yelled, "What?!" holding out my hand until he surrendered the offending coins. He may not have been able to keep track of his schedule, his plane tickets, his overstuffed briefcase or his socks, but he could, on any given day, absorb Henry Mintzberg's brilliant broken-window theory, Donna Williams's description of autism, Alice Munro's newest collection of short stories or Ralph Klein's hold on Albertans. And he'd do all this before most people had even thought about what they might eat for lunch. I decided early on that whatever he couldn't keep track of, I would, and that might free up more of his brain to focus on other, well, grander things.

An actual job description never existed (for instance, a few weeks after I started, Peter said, "Oh, by the way, did I mention I've got this little golf tournament?"). Everywhere I went, people would ask me what I did at *Morningside*. By extension, they were also wondering what all the talented, resourceful, unbelievably dedicated, smart producers at *Morningside* – and their network counterparts across the country – did for the show. I would explain that producers thought of the story ideas, came up with a focus, booked the guests, wrote the background, did the research, scripted the outline of questions – and that's just the beginning. The questioner would nod. Even my parents, bless them, couldn't figure out what I – what we – did all day. To them, I believe, the program sounded as if Peter went in every morning and called up a bunch of people he felt like talking to that day. That did not dismay us – if that's how the listener thought the program worked, then we knew we had done our job well. And even though Peter talked about his producers every chance he got, publicly and in print, and read our names every Friday at the end of the week's programming, we were, are, largely invisible. And that's exactly as it should be.

Unlike most of the others, though, I was lucky enough to do many events and projects with Peter outside *Morningside*. The most important projects were the golf tournaments. They were started at the behest of John O'Leary, who is now the president of Frontier College. The first was held at the Briars, Peter's home course in Ontario. They spread – to Ottawa, then Victoria, then to every province and territory – because lovely like-minded (meaning nutty, but in a good way) people wanted to organize something to celebrate and raise money for literacy.

Before Peter and I stopped going to every single one, we had travelled to 121 tournaments, zipping across the country for three months every spring and summer in a kind of continuous "checking in" with everyone. He didn't just link the country on the radio every day; he was also a visible presence, linking a phalanx of people – musicians, captains of industry, poets, literacy workers, learners, volunteers, politicians, authors. He loved this part most of all, I think. The CEOs of the Royal Bank and Quaker Oats and Superior Propane sitting enthralled as Bronwen Wallace or Susan Musgrave delivered a poem; David Peterson coming out of the audience to turn the pages for a newly elected Bob Rae to play the piano; musicians so inspired after hearing a learner tell her story that new songs were composed. Introductions made, relationships formed, and another map of the country – the *Morningside* map, the PGI map – created. I'd venture to say not a place remained untouched by one or the other.

And the delight he got out of it all. The breathtaking helicopter ride over the Liard River after the first tournament in Watson Lake, Yukon, when Peter asked the pilot: "How the hell did you get permission to carve this golf course into the side of a mountain?" and the answer was, "Well, up here, it's easier to get forgiveness than permission." Or later that day, when he welled up reading "Love You Forever" while Cynthia Dale sang along beside him. His amazement when we started to do annual golf tournaments with the Assembly of First Nations for Aboriginal Languages and everybody called everybody else "chief." (It was a gathering of the chiefs, and they all really were chiefs.) His laughter the evening of the first Red Barn, when I was looking for W.O. Mitchell to do a sound check and Peter overheard Patsy Pehleman say W.O. was likely out in back of the barn, "looking for the wind."

I wish you could have been with us when we waited in Calgary with 150 golfers for two inches of snow to melt on the tees while Valdy's songs kept us warm until the sun rose over the brilliant yellows of an Alberta autumn. Or travelling back and forth and back and forth on the ferry between Halifax and Dartmouth with then mayor of Dartmouth John Savage (that's where he held the meeting – in the harbour), who was laying out his plan to bring the golf tournaments for literacy to Nova Scotia. Or fly fishing with Frank McKenna and the fabulous insane Kenny family, cigars in hand, waders on, in the Miramichi. Those are all famous names, but the trips and golf tournaments and remote broadcasts were filled to bursting with fishermen and oil drillers, farmers and potters, writers and parents, university students, recent immigrants and loggers, activists and business people – ordinary Canadians, and yet not an ordinary person among them.

Extraordinary stories. Compelling lives. Every Labour Day a new radio season would start, and there was never a concern that there were enough people left that Peter hadn't met, or enough new stories to discover, to fill the months ahead. It was, is, endless. There is a curious notion among a tiny group of people that the Canada Peter reflected on *Morningside* didn't really exist, that he was perpetuating a myth. That's so silly. Of course it's there. Do you think he made up those people and their stories and their letters? They're the tip of the iceberg.

∾

Fifteen years of mail is still around – you can go read it yourself. Trent University, one of Peter's last and most loved homes, holds his papers. I know what is in those dozens of boxes. After the thousands of letters, the most telling will be the envelopes that say "PG: Bulletin Board Season 1991–92," "93–94," and so on. Every season, Peter started with a virgin bulletin board (excepting the sign "As Canadian as possible under the circumstances," the result of the now infamous contest to finish the phrase, which stayed put). As the season progressed, he added things that came in the mail, or from his family, or the paper, that really struck him. On the last day of each season, I emptied the board, put everything in an envelope and labelled it. Those envelopes hold the clue to everything you might not know about Peter: what he was sentimental about, what made him laugh, what kept him going. Pictures of Krista Munro's miracle baby, a letter from his cousin Deborah Martin, a fax from his daughter Alison or from PSB (always signed with a drawing of a martini glass), a miniature pair of handcrafted kamiks from Rankin, postcards from afar, editorial cartoons. That bulletin board was the microcosm of what the show became to many – the community bulletin board for the nation. What *Morningside* became – what Peter did – was to become a part of the fabric of the nation, a fabric that, Peter knew, existed already. This insinuation into lives that already existed was made possible partly because Peter understood that listening to the radio is not like watching television. Radio means you invite a person into your morning – or afternoon or Saturday night. That person is welcomed into your kitchen, your car, your bedroom and your life, to keep you company while you do something else – cooking, driving, working. As the letters in this book and over the years attest, people don't listen to a program or a service or a network. People listen to a person. If they trust him, they will listen to whatever and whomever that person brings. They want a personality – a friend, a companion, an advocate, someone to make an introduction. They want a host; they want a star.

There was a move afoot, after Peter Gzowski left CBC Radio, to get beyond that notion. While many listeners (and producers) were desperate for the next Peter Gzowski, management seemed to want anything but. No stars, no overriding personalities. Although it's true the CBC gave Peter the platform – three hours of daily national radio is nothing to sneeze at – it was the listener who gave him the power he earned and deserved. They gave it to him because he consistently reflected what they – we – wanted to know, or brought the people and events they were hungry to hear. Peter engaged us in our own and our neighbour's issues, lives, triumphs, problems, talents and decisions. The true stakeholder – the listener – gave Peter his mantle, and he took the honour very, very seriously.

When *Morningside* ended, we went, at Peter's request, to where he believed he began, to Moose Jaw. Elsewhere in this book and in countless articles and pieces of tape, listeners, contributors and producers have tried to grasp the gravity of that day. I can't. We did the show live very early in the morning from the lobby of the old Harwood Hotel. Hearing Bill Mitchell's voice (for the last time) as he said goodbye to Peter, and to *Morningside*, was about all any of us could take.

The next day, at a party conceived of and paid for by Peter, everyone who ever worked on *Morningside* was invited to board a boat in Toronto harbour for a four-hour tour. After some organization and a lot of drunken and hilarious choreography, many of my fellow colleagues, at least the women, gave the performance of our lives. On bended knee and meaning every damn syllable we belted out at the top of our lungs all the verses of "To Sir With Love."

It's hard to believe he's gone. And, in many ways, he's not. The map remains; the relationships forged by and through him continue. He is, in a way, everywhere.

SHELLEY AMBROSE

Contributors, in Order of Appearance

Gill Howard, Toronto
Shelagh Rogers, Eden Mills, Ontario
Ron Karras, Montreal
Robert Fulford, Toronto
Trish Clair Peck, London, Ontario
David Staines, Ottawa
Silver Donald Cameron, D'Escousse, Nova Scotia
Bonnie Baker Cowan, Toronto
Keri Smith, Flesherton, Ontario
Chris Czajkowski, Nimpo Lake, British Columbia
Judi Conacher, Toronto
Kim Hunter, Nepean, Ontario
Sandra McCulloch, Cobble Hill, British Columbia
Heather Ferris, Vanderhoof, British Columbia
Laurie Allan, Grimsby, Ontario
Sue Campbell, Toronto
Doug Gibson, Toronto
The Reverend Iain Macdonald, Halifax
Val Ross, Toronto
Elizabeth Baird, Toronto
Bruce Skilliter, Kindersley, Saskatchewan
Valerie Walker, Calgary
Peter H. Breau, Shediac, New Brunswick
Douglas Ward, Ottawa
Jane Forner, Mill Bay, Vancouver Island
Michael Enright, Toronto
Alice Munro, Clinton, Ontario, and Comox, British Columbia
Amy Bennet, Big Lots, Nova Scotia
Dave Shaw, Glenwood, Newfoundland
Pat Buckna, Port Coquitlam, British Columbia
Allan Goddard, Almonte, Ontario

Ross Driedger, via e-mail
Nicole Bélanger, Montreal
Leesa Alldred, West
    Vancouver
Mar Penner Griswold, Fort
    Erie, Ontario
Bruce Marsh, East York,
    Ontario
Gordon Hebert, Montreal
Rick MacLean, Summerside,
    Prince Edward Island
Stephen Couchman, Toronto
Graeme McDonald, Dorval,
    Quebec
Susie Doyle, Timberlea, Nova
    Scotia
Rauld Liset, New
    Westminster, British
    Columbia
Les MacPherson, Saskatoon
Lesley Moffatt, Red Deer,
    Alberta
Valerie Loewen, Whitehorse,
    Yukon
Monny Rutabagas, Victoria
Dianne L. Martin, Toronto
Joan Baxter Bamako, Mali,
    West Africa
Andy Wood, Toronto
Hugh Williamson, Halifax
Shari Graydon, Vancouver
Cindy Schultz, Halifax
Ted Gooden, London,
    Ontario

David Shaw, Toronto
Nancy White, Toronto
Susan Mundy, Lower
    Sackville, Nova Scotia
Pepper Mintz, Ottawa
Doug Edmond, Winnipeg
Barbara Mercer, Upper Island
    Cove, Newfoundland
Erin Lemon, Kingston,
    Ontario
Lisa (Kowaltschuk) Noble,
    Hastings, Ontario
Marieke Meyer, Toronto
Katherine Macklem, Toronto
Ian Pearson, Toronto
Patsy Pehleman, Toronto
June Callwood, Toronto
Cathy Anderson, Regina
Elizabeth Gray, Toronto
Meredith Levine, Toronto
Bonnie Stern, Toronto
Tom Jokinen, Toronto
Sean Prpick, Regina
Douglas Knight, Toronto
Spider Robinson, Bowen
    Island, British Columbia
Rex Murphy, Toronto
Anne Bayin, Toronto
Mary Young Leckie, Toronto
Rick Mercer, Halifax
Anna Fraser, Eureka, Nova
    Scotia
Dean Whiting, via e-mail
Terre Nash, Montreal

Martina Payette, Airdrie,
Alberta
Emily Campbell, Regina
Sean Malby, Toronto
Kathryn Davies, Newmarket,
Ontario
Krista Munroe, Medicine Hat,
Alberta
Lois Addison, Dunrobin,
Ontario
John Firth, Ottawa
Laurie Stephenson, Head of
Saint Mary's Bay, Nova
Scotia
Bill McLean, London,
Ontario
Adele Farough, Ottawa
Michael Myers, Regina
Owen McDermott, via
e-mail
Barbara Campbell, Palgrave,
Ontario
Jack Vander Hoek, Ottawa
Mark Wilson, New Liskeard,
Ontario
Craig Wilson, via e-mail
Penny Simpson, Burnaby,
British Columbia
Barry Bucknell, Grande
Prairie, Alberta
The Reverend Christopher
White, Oshawa, Ontario
Frank McKenna, Moncton,
New Brunswick

Brian Ham, via e-mail
Merle Elgert, Edmonton
Jim Duggan, French River,
Prince Edward Island
Alex Houghton, Ottawa
Sid Andrews, Gananoque,
Ontario
Dalton Camp
Judith Gunderson, Kelowna,
British Columbia
The Nunavut Literacy
Council: Sandy Kusugak,
Dan Page, Debbie
Menchions, Sue Ball, Julia
Ogina, Elizabeth Lyall,
Candace Wiwcharyk,
Maggie Putulik, Shuvinai
Mike, Kim Crockatt, Cayla
Chenier, Janet Onalik
Catherine Pellerin,
Yellowknife
Paul Andrew, Yellowknife
John B. Lee, Brantford,
Ontario
Lynn Fogwill and Barb
Paquin, Yellowknife
Mindy Willett, Kugluktuk,
Nunavut
Jacquelyn Thayer Scott, Ben
Eoin, Cape Breton, Nova
Scotia
Tom Stewart, Kugluktuk,
Nunavut
Murd Nicholson, Yukon

René Fumoleau, Lutsel'ke,
  Great Slave Lake,
  Northwest Territories
Debbie Peters, Whitehorse,
  Yukon
Lorne Rubenstein, Toronto
Joe and Jane Dragon,
  Yellowknife
Stephen Kakfwi, Yellowknife
John O'Leary, Toronto
John MacLachlan Gray,
  Vancouver
Jennifer Davidson, Waterloo,
  Ontario
Sasha Furlani, Toronto
Lynda Mannik, Peterborough,
  Ontario
Avie Bennett, Toronto
David Wallbridge, via e-mail
Bonnie Patterson,
  Peterborough, Ontario
Gene McKeiver,
  Peterborough, Ontario
Margie Davenport, via e-mail
Joni Brunton, Stouffville,
  Ontario

Leisha LeCouvie, Montreal
Deborah van Wyck, Montreal
Kathie M. Leece, via e-mail
Jodi Aoki and Bernadette
  Dodge, Peterborough,
  Ontario
Jack Madden, Sutton, Ontario
Stuart McLean, Toronto
Tom Jackson, Calgary
Bob Bossin, Gabriola Island,
  British Columbia
Cindy Church, Toronto
Joan Besen, Toronto
John Girvin, London
Roch Carrier, Ottawa
Mick Gzowski, Toronto
Michele Landsberg, Toronto
Pauline Pariser, Toronto
Sheree Fitch, River John,
  Nova Scotia
Murray McLauchlan, Toronto
Shelley Ambrose, Toronto
Susan Aglukark, Toronto

Acknowledgements

Thanks to the following publications and writers who have generously granted permission to use previously published material:

Bernadette Dodge and Jodi Aoki, "Dear Peter," Trent University Archives *News*, Number 2, June 2002, pp. 2-3.

Bonnie Baker Cowan, "Editing Peter," *CARPNews FiftyPlus* Magazine, April 2002.

Bonnie Stern, "Remembering some of Gzowski's favourite recipes," from the *National Post*, 16 February 2002.

Dalton Camp, "Peter's love for Canada will be his legacy to us," from the *Toronto Star*, 27 January 2002. Reprinted with permission – The Toronto Star Syndicate.

Doug Gibson, "Remembering Peter Gzowski," *Quill & Quire*, March 2002.

Elizabeth Gray, "It wasn't just his voice; when he laughed, the audience joined in," from the *Toronto Star*, 27 January 2002.

June Callwood, "Vox Populi/Peter Gzowski, 1934–2002," in *Time* Magazine, 4 February 2002, p. 46.

Katherine Macklem, "The Sage in the Corner," from *Maclean's*, 4 February 2002, p. 22; reprinted by permission from *Maclean's* Magazine.

Les MacPherson, "Professionalism made Gzowski legendary," Saskatoon *StarPhoenix*, 26 January 2002, p. A3.

Lorne Rubenstein, "Gzowski tourneys form truly Canadian tour," from the *Globe and Mail*, 2 February 2002, p. S1.

Michael Enright, Cover Story, from *Maclean's*, 4 February 2002.

Michele Landsberg, "Gzowski's addiction was complex and deadly," from the *Toronto Star*, 2 February 2002. Reprinted with permission – The Toronto Star Syndicate.

Murd Nicholson, from the Learners in ACTION newsletter, February, 2002.

Murray McLauchlan, "Saying Goodbye," reprinted by permission of the songwriter.

Rex Murphy, "Pythons, misfits and Canadians – Gzowski talked to us all," from the *Globe and Mail*, 2 February 2002, p. A19.

Rick McLean, from the Miramichi *Leader*, 29 January 2002.

Robert Fulford, "He had the courage to be scared," from the *National Post*, 25 January 2002.

Roch Carrier, "*Hommage* to Peter Gzowski," *Feliciter* (Canadian Library Association), No. 2, 2002, p. 58.

Silver Donald Cameron, "Missing Peter Gzowski," from the Halifax *Chronicle-Herald*, 27 January, 2002; reprinted with permission from Paper Tiger Enterprises.

Spider Robinson, Cover Story, from the *Globe and Mail*, 31 January 2002.

Tom Jackson, "Goodbye old friend," from *InterActra*, February 2002.